KATHARINE HEPBURN

KATHARINE HEPBURN

CAROLINE LATHAM

CHELSEA HOUSE PUBLISHERS

PHILADELPHIA

EDITOR-IN-CHIEF: Nancy Toff
EXECUTIVE EDITOR: Remmel T. Nunn
MANAGING EDITOR: Karyn Gullen Browne
COPY CHIEF: Juliann Barbato
PICTURE EDITOR: Adrian G. Allen
ART DIRECTOR: Giannella Garrett
MANUFACTURING MANAGER: Gerald Levine

Staff for KATHARINE HEPBURN

SENIOR EDITOR: Elisa Petrini
ASSISTANT EDITOR: Maria Behan
EDITORIAL ASSISTANT: Theodore Keyes
COPYEDITORS: James Guiry and Ellen Scordato
PICTURE RESEARCHER: Diane Moroff
DESIGNER: Design Oasis
PRODUCTION COORDINATOR: Joseph Romano
COVER ILLUSTRATION: Alan J. Nahigian

The Chelsea House World Wide Web site address is
http://www.chelseahouse.com

9 8

Library of Congress Cataloging in Publication Data

Latham, Caroline. KATHARINE HEPBURN

(American women of achievement)
Bibliography: p.
Includes index.
1. Hepburn, Katharine, 1909–   —Juvenile literature.
2. Actors—United States—Biography—Juvenile literature.
[1. Hepburn, Katharine, 1909–   . 2. Actors and actresses]
I Title. II. Series.
PN2287.H45L37   1987   791.43'028'0924 [B] [92]   87-8023

ISBN 1-55546-658-3
     0-7910-0416-3 (pbk.)

CONTENTS

AMERICAN WOMEN OF ACHIEVEMENT

Abigail Adams
women's rights advocate

Jane Addams
social worker

Louisa May Alcott
author

Marian Anderson
singer

Susan B. Anthony
woman suffragist

Ethel Barrymore
actress

Clara Barton
founder of the American Red Cross

Elizabeth Blackwell
physician

Nellie Bly
journalist

Margaret Bourke-White
photographer

Pearl Buck
author

Rachel Carson
biologist and author

Mary Cassatt
artist

Agnes De Mille
choreographer

Emily Dickinson
poet

Isadora Duncan
dancer

Amelia Earhart
aviator

Mary Baker Eddy
founder of the Christian Science church

Betty Friedan
feminist

Althea Gibson
tennis champion

Emma Goldman
political activist

Helen Hayes
actress

Lillian Hellman
playwright

Katharine Hepburn
actress

Karen Horney
psychoanalyst

Anne Hutchinson
religious leader

Mahalia Jackson
gospel singer

Helen Keller
humanitarian

Jeane Kirkpatrick
diplomat

Emma Lazarus
poet

Clare Boothe Luce
author and diplomat

Barbara McClintock
biologist

Margaret Mead
anthropologist

Edna St. Vincent Millay
poet

Julia Morgan
architect

Grandma Moses
painter

Louise Nevelson
sculptor

Sandra Day O'Connor
Supreme Court justice

Georgia O'Keeffe
painter

Eleanor Roosevelt
diplomat and humanitarian

Wilma Rudolph
champion athlete

Florence Sabin
medical researcher

Beverly Sills
opera singer

Gertrude Stein
author

Gloria Steinem
feminist

Harriet Beecher Stowe
author and abolitionist

Mae West
entertainer

Edith Wharton
author

Phillis Wheatley
poet

Babe Didrikson Zaharias
champion athlete

CHELSEA HOUSE PUBLISHERS

"Remember the Ladies"

MATINA S. HORNER

Remember the Ladies." That is what Abigail Adams wrote to her husband John, then a delegate to the Continental Congress, as the Founding Fathers met in Philadelphia to form a new nation in March of 1776. "Be more generous and favorable to them than your ancestors. Do not put such unlimited power in the hands of the Husbands. If particular care and attention is not paid to the Ladies," Abigail Adams warned, "we are determined to foment a Rebellion, and will not hold ourselves bound by any Laws in which we have no voice, or Representation."

The words of Abigail Adams, one of the earliest American advocates of women's rights, were prophetic. Because when we have not "remembered the ladies," they have, by their words and deeds, reminded us so forcefully of the omission that we cannot fail to remember them. For the history of American women is as interesting and varied as the history of our nation as a whole. American women have played an integral part in founding, settling, and building our country. Some we remember as remarkable women who—against great odds—achieved distinction in the public arena: Anne Hutchinson, who in the 17th century became a charismatic religious leader; Phillis Wheatley, an 18th-century black slave who became a poet; Susan B. Anthony, whose name is synonymous with the 19th-century women's rights movement, and who led the struggle to enfranchise women; and, in our own century, Amelia Earhart, the first woman to cross the Atlantic Ocean by air.

These extraordinary women certainly merit our admiration, but other women, "common women," many of them all but forgotten, should also be recognized for their contributions to American thought and culture. Women have been community builders; they have founded schools and formed voluntary associations to help those in need; they have assumed the major responsibility for rearing children, passing on from one generation to the next the values that keep a culture alive. These and innumerable other contributions, once ignored, are now being recognized by scholars, students, and the public. It is exciting and gratifying to realize that a part of our history that was hardly acknowledged a few generations ago is now being studied and brought to light.

In recent decades, the field of women's history has grown from obscurity to a politically controversial splinter movement to academic respectability, in many cases mainstreamed into such traditional disciplines as history, economics, and psychology. Scholars of women, both female and male, have organized research centers at such prestigious institutions as Wellesley College, Stanford University, and the University of California. Other notable centers for women's studies are the Center for the American Woman and Politics at the Eagleton Institute of Politics at Rutgers University, the Henry A. Murray Research Center for the Study of Lives, at Radcliffe College, and the Women's Research and Education Institute, the research arm of the Congressional Caucus on Women's Issues. Other scholars and public figures have established archives and libraries, such as the Schlesinger Library on the History of Women in America, at Radcliffe College, and the Sophia Smith Collection, at Smith College, to collect and preserve the written and tangible legacies of women.

From the initial donation of the Women's Rights Collection in 1943, the Schlesinger Library grew to encompass vast collections documenting the manifold accomplishments of American women. Simultaneously, the women's movement in general and the academic discipline of women's studies in particular also began with a narrow definition and gradually expanded their mandate. Early causes such as woman suffrage and social reform, abolition and organized labor were joined by newer concerns such as the history of women in business and the professions and in politics and government; the study of the family; and social issues such as health policy and education.

Women, as historian Arthur M. Schlesinger, jr., once pointed out, "have constituted the most spectacular casualty of traditional history. They have made up at least half the human race, but you could never tell that by looking at the books historians write." The new breed of historians is remedying that omission. They have written books about immigrant women and about working-class women who struggled for survival in cities and about black women who met the challenges of life in rural areas. They are telling the stories of women who, despite the barriers of tradition and economics, became lawyers and doctors and public figures.

The women's studies movement has also led scholars to question traditional interpretations of their respective disciplines. For example, the study of war has traditionally been an exercise in military and political analysis, an examination of strategies planned and executed by men. But scholars of women's history have pointed out that wars have also been periods of tremendous change and even opportunity for women, because the very absence of men on the home front enabled them to expand their educational, economic, and professional activities and to assume leadership in their homes.

The early scholars of women's history showed a unique brand of courage in choosing to investigate new subjects and take new approaches to old ones. Often, like their subjects, they endured criticism and even ostracism by their academic colleagues. But their efforts have unquestionably been worthwhile, because with the publication of each new study and book another piece of the historical patchwork is sewn into place, revealing an increasingly comprehensive picture of the role of women in our rich and varied history.

Such books on groups of women are essential, but books that focus on the lives of individuals are equally indispensable. Biographies can be inspirational, offering their readers the example of people with vision who have looked outside themselves for their goals and have often struggled against great obstacles to achieve them. Marian Anderson, for instance, had to overcome racial bigotry in order to perfect her art and perform as a concert singer. Isadora Duncan defied the rules of classical dance to find true artistic freedom. Jane Addams had to break down society's notions of the proper role for women in order to create new social institutions, notably the settlement house. All of these women had to come to terms both with themselves and with the world in which they lived. Only then could they move ahead as pioneers in their chosen callings.

Biography can inspire not only by adulation but also by realism. It helps us to see not only the qualities in others that we hope to emulate, but also, perhaps, the weaknesses that made them "human." By helping us identify with the subject on a more personal level they help us to feel that we, too, can achieve such goals. We read about Eleanor Roosevelt, for instance, who occupied a unique and seemingly enviable position as the wife of the president. Yet we can sympathize with her inner dilemma: an inherently shy woman, she had to force herself to live a most public life in order to use her position to benefit others. We may not be able to imagine ourselves having the immense poetic talent of Emily Dickinson, but from her story we can understand the challenges faced by a creative woman who was expected to fulfill many family responsibilities. And though few of us will ever reach the level of athletic accomplishment displayed by Wilma Rudolph or Babe Zaharias, we can still appreciate their spirit, their overwhelming will to excel.

A biography is a multifaceted lens. It is first of all a magnification, the intimate examination of one particular life. But at the same time, it is a wide-angle lens, informing us about the world in which the subject lived. We come away from reading about one life knowing more about the social, political, and economic fabric of the time. It is for this reason, perhaps, that the great New England essayist Ralph Waldo Emerson wrote, in 1841, "There is properly no history: only biography." And it is also why biography, and particularly women's biography, will continue to fascinate writers and readers alike.

KATHARINE HEPBURN

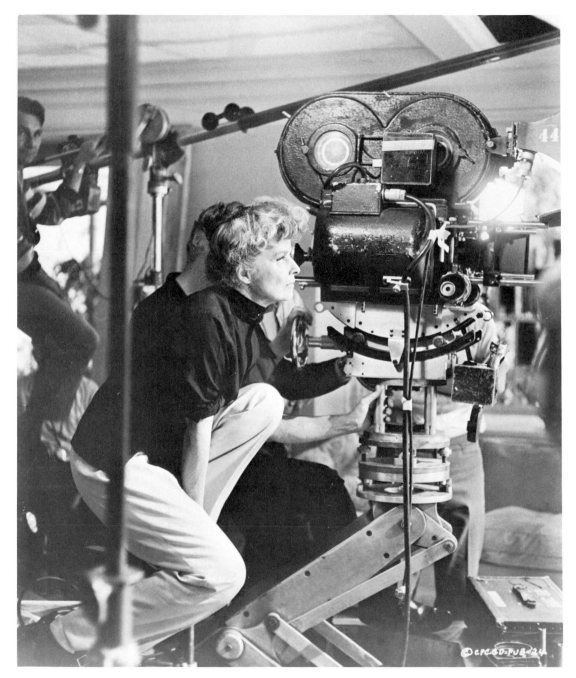

Returning to the screen after a five-year absence, Katharine Hepburn checks a camera angle on the set of 1967's Guess Who's Coming to Dinner?

ONE

Return of the Renegade

On February 15, 1967, Katharine Hepburn—an actress notorious for her rabid dislike of photographers and reporters—gave a press conference at New York City's plush Waldorf-Astoria Hotel. For the past five years, the public had heard virtually nothing from the athletic redhead who had propelled herself to stardom by playing characters that were extensions of her own vibrant personality, characters who shared her genteel wit and straightforward intelligence. Conflicting rumors about her odd "disappearance" had abounded, and Hepburn, who had always been something of an enigma, seemed to be slipping into obscurity.

Yet here she was, fielding questions, gracefully deflecting intrusions into her well-guarded private realm—and charming everyone in sight. Well aware of her reputation, the reporters had ex-

pected Hepburn simply to read a brief prepared speech. Instead, she chatted amiably with the press for two hours. The 57-year-old actress told the astonished journalists, "Most people get grumpier in their old age; I get nicer."

Hepburn had indeed mellowed since she first stormed Hollywood in 1932, but now her purpose was more serious than breaking her press silence. Hepburn had called the conference to announce the beginning of a project that held tremendous importance for her: a new film on the highly controversial topic of race relations.

For more than a decade, America had been torn apart by social conflict and racially motivated violence. There was discrimination against blacks in virtually every area of life, sometimes as a matter of law. In the American South, blacks often could not eat in the

Police officers round up looters during the racially motivated Newark, New Jersey, riot of 1967, which left 26 dead and 1,500 injured. Guess Who's Coming to Dinner?, *released that same year, was Hepburn's attempt to promote racial harmony.*

same restaurants as whites, use the same bathrooms or drinking fountains, or attend white schools and colleges. Many southern blacks were denied their right to vote as well. In the North, although laws were more liberal, blacks still suffered discrimination in housing, education, and employment.

A civil rights movement had arisen to fight for black equality, and many discriminatory laws were struck down by the Civil Rights Act of 1964. But abuses persisted, and certain white groups such as the Ku Klux Klan, who resented black gains, launched vicious attacks on blacks and civil rights activists. Events would come to a head in the summer of 1967, when race riots broke out in 127 cities across the nation.

Because Hepburn considered civil rights such a critical issue, she had decided to return to the screen. Her co-stars in the new film—to be called

In a scene from Guess Who's Coming to Dinner?, *Christina Drayton (Hepburn) discusses the future with her daughter (Katharine Houghton) and her future son-in-law (Sidney Poitier).*

Guess Who's Coming to Dinner?—would be Sidney Poitier; her niece, novice actress Katharine Houghton; and Spencer Tracy, who had been Hepburn's frequent partner, both on-screen and off, for more than a quarter of a century.

Spencer Tracy was the reason that Hepburn, famous for the number and variety of roles she tackled, had not worked since 1962. The actor had long been in failing health, and Hepburn had withdrawn from her thriving film and stage career to care for him. But in late 1966, when producer-director Stanley Kramer approached them with the script for *Guess Who's Coming to Dinner?*, both actors had been intrigued. The film would use humor to explore how even well-intentioned people practice racism. Nonetheless, Hepburn had hesitated to accept the offer, fearing the stress of filmmaking might threaten Tracy's life. As Hepburn

Hepburn and Spencer Tracy embrace in their first movie together, 1942's Woman of the Year. *Gossip columnist Hedda Hopper was on the mark when she hinted that the film's love scenes "look like the real thing."*

biographer Charles Higham wrote, "Making *Guess Who's Coming to Dinner?* became an enormous task of courage for everyone connected with it. Spencer knew he was risking his life to make it. Kate was risking losing him.

Kramer was risking his bank balance and his career. Yet everyone felt so passionately that the WASP [White Anglo-Saxon Protestant] public needed to be jolted out of its anti-black bias that they went ahead with a total and dedicated commitment to the material."

Characteristically, once Hepburn made her decision, she was determined to see the project through. "She's that kind of remarkable woman," said Kramer. When Columbia Pictures was unable to obtain insurance for the movie because of Tracy's frail health, she and Kramer saved the project by agreeing that their salaries would revert to the studio if the film was left unfinished.

The plot of *Guess Who's Coming to Dinner?* revolves around the reaction of two sets of parents—one black, the other white—to the news that their children are getting married. Hepburn and Tracy played the liberal, socially prominent mother and father of a white woman who has fallen in love with a black doctor. Suddenly, their abstract belief in racial equality is *really* challenged. But by the film's end, they accept their daughter's fiancé and reaffirm their opposition to all forms of bigotry.

Hepburn plunged into her role as the liberal mother with her renowned professional drive. She offered suggestions to the director, hairdressers, and technical crews alike. Kramer remembered, "She had to run free, with and around a director. She was always creative, one of the two or three most creative artists I've ever worked with."

Kramer found Hepburn's energy on the set equally amazing. He recalled,

"She was a driving worker. Work, work, work. She can work till everybody drops." Some of the most difficult scenes were those in which the actors played to blank space, because many scenes were shot around Tracy to avoid taxing his strength. This must have been especially upsetting for Hepburn, but she triumphed over this obstacle as she did most others—through sheer willpower.

For all Hepburn's disciplined toughness, *Guess Who's Coming to Dinner?* also revealed the gentleness she had acquired over the years. She had faced many personal and professional crises in her career, and they had left their mark. As Stanley Kramer put it, "She has learned softness from the privilege of failure." Hepburn was strikingly forceful in scenes in which her character fought against bigotry; undeniably moving when her character called a truce and showed tenderness.

Although the movie set out to make a social statement, it was also a love story played by two actors whose personal histories added depth to their scenes together. No longer young, Hepburn and Tracy still fought with the same wit and conviction that had been their trademark in their eight previous films together. And when they stopped fighting, the strength of their personal relationship made their on-screen reconciliations especially tender.

On the last day of filming, everyone

Guess Who's Coming to Dinner? *was Hepburn's last collaboration with Tracy, her longtime screen partner and life companion.*

concerned felt a mixture of pride and relief. Pride in their accomplishment, relief that the long days of hard work were over—and that Tracy had survived. Hepburn made a speech expressing her gratitude to the film crew. Speaking for herself and Tracy, she told them "I don't think you people realize how dependent we are on you for the encouragement you give us. These are the things that make up our lives."

During the shooting Hepburn had told a journalist, "It's hard to make what people call a comeback, you know. . . . In this business, people just forget you." But the movie's astounding box office success soon proved that no one had forgotten Katharine Hepburn; it became the most popular film of her career and eventually sold more than $25 million worth of tickets.

The film was indeed Hepburn and Tracy's last collaboration and won them both Academy Award nominations. Hepburn was in France shooting a movie on the night of the awards presentation. When she learned she had won the Best Actress award, her only response was to ask, "Did Mr. Tracy win too?" Hearing that he had not, she replied, "That's okay. I'm sure mine is for the two of us."

Although *Guess Who's Coming to Dinner?* does not seem radical today, at the time some people were amazed that a well-respected actress would star in such a controversial picture. After the film's release, Hepburn dismissed those who attacked the film and her involvement in it. "I suppose it will disturb some people and raise a fuss, but fifty or a hundred years from now, I don't think this picture will be shocking at all, because we'll be practicing intermarriage."

Remarks such as this one only further inflamed her critics, but they should not have been surprised at Hepburn's outspokenness, nor at her decision to become involved in such a ground-breaking film as *Guess Who's Coming to Dinner?* in the first place. She has a long tradition of acting on her convictions—even on unpopular ones. Hepburn has been a renegade from the very start.

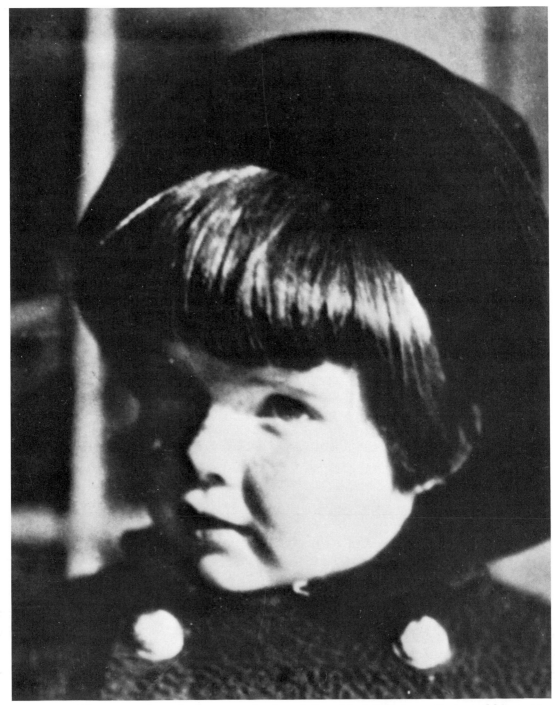

Four-year-old Kate Hepburn had not yet developed the chiseled features that would become her trademark in later years. Born in 1909, she was fascinated by the era's silent films and fantasized about becoming a movie star.

TWO

The Young Katharine Hepburn

Katharine Hepburn once told an interviewer, "I had the most wonderful childhood."

Born on November 8, 1909, in Hartford, Connecticut, she was the second child in a family that eventually included six children, three boys and three girls. All of them were excellent athletes, and Kate, as her family called her, was no exception. At an early age, she learned to figure skate, to swim and dive gracefully, to play a good game of golf and tennis—even to wrestle and master the trapeze. She was especially devoted to her brother Tom, the oldest and liveliest of the children. Kate did her best to keep up with him, even though he was six years older. She soon became notorious around Hartford as a tomboy who asked people to

call her "Jimmy" and insisted her hair be cut short so it would not be a bother during wrestling matches.

Young Kate's parents encouraged her athletic development because they thought it made her more independent. As she later joked, "I really was not brought up to feel that women were underdogs. I was totally unaware that we were the second-rate sex." The Hepburns taught their daughter to stand up for her beliefs, and they themselves set a good example. Her father, Thomas Norval Hepburn, the son of an Episcopalian minister, had studied medicine at Johns Hopkins University in Baltimore, Maryland. Moved by the suffering of a patient, he decided to specialize in the treatment of venereal disease at a time when most members

Hepburn's mother, "Kit," defends birth control before the House Judiciary Committee in 1945. Her liberal beliefs scandalized the family's conservative Hartford, Connecticut neighbors.

of polite society refused to acknowledge the existence of sexually transmitted illnesses.

While he was still in school, Thomas Hepburn met and married Katharine Houghton, known as "Kit," a young woman from one of New England's most illustrious families. Like her husband, Kit Hepburn listened more to her own conscience than to public opinion. She appalled conservative Hartford, where the family settled, by working for controversial causes, in-

cluding birth control and women's suffrage. She had a reputation for grilling new acquaintances on their political opinions as soon as they were introduced and dismissing conservatives by muttering, "How dull, how awfully dull!"

The Hepburns sought out a more stimulating circle of friends, including militant feminist Emmeline Pankhurst; anarchist Emma Goldman, who advocated the abolition of all governments; and novelist Sinclair Lewis, who scandalized America with his frank portraits of small-town life. Looking back on her parents' marriage, Katharine Hepburn remembers their union as joyous, if not quite peaceful, "They never argued about things—my mother never wanted 'things' the way most people do—they only argued about ideas."

Mrs. Hepburn often brought her children along to political meetings and demonstrations. Young Kate carried signs and handed out leaflets. She later reflected, "I learned early what it is to be snubbed for a good cause. Snobbery has never worried me since."

Although the Hepburns allowed their children many freedoms and openly discussed such topics as politics and sexuality with them, they did not believe in letting their children run wild. If Kate got into one too many scrapes, she would be spanked or sent to take an ice-cold bath. "Those baths were responsible for my later perversity," Hepburn once reminisced. "They gave me the impression that the more bitter the medicine, the better it was for you. That may be the reason I came to think that the more insulting the press was, the more it stimulated me."

Until she was 10 years old, Katharine Hepburn's primary problems were her red hair and freckles, which she considered unattractive. Then, on Easter Sunday 1920, tragedy struck the Hepburn family. A few days earlier, Kate and her brother Tom had been taken to see the play *A Connecticut Yankee in King Arthur's Court*, in which a character avoids death by tightening his neck muscles during a hanging. When Kate went to awaken Tom on Easter morning, she was surprised to find her brother missing from his room. After a long search, she found Tom's lifeless body hanging from the attic rafters. The loss of her adored brother, and the horrifying circumstances of his death, cast a shadow over the rest of her childhood.

After Tom's death, Kate became moody and withdrawn. Because playacting was one of the few things that lifted her spirits, the Hepburns encouraged her first forays into the world of the theater. She played the title role in a backyard production of *Bluebeard* with relish and starred as the beast in *Beauty and the Beast*. This second play marked the emergence of young Kate's social conscience: She decided to charge admission and to devote the proceeds to the Navajo Indians, whose financial hardships had been described to her by a missionary.

That same year, when Kate was 10, her parents decided to withdraw her from the public school system. Considering her headstrong nature, they thought she would learn more if she was tutored at home. Kate was quite happy with the new setup, especially because it allowed her to schedule les-

According to a family friend, the teenage Katharine Hepburn was "shy—not in the ordinary sense, but with a profound basic shyness that was hidden under an arrogant front."

Thanks to her rigorous tutoring, Katharine Hepburn entered college before she reached her 16th birthday. She attended Bryn Mawr, a prestigious women's college near Philadelphia, Pennsylvania. Naturally abashed by the strange new experience of dealing with other students, Kate concealed her fearfulness behind a haughty demeanor. Making her first appearance in the college dining room, the young redhead strode in and took her seat as if she were a member of royalty. Her confident veneer was quickly shattered when one of the girls sized her up and remarked, "Ah, self-conscious beauty!" Kate ran from the dining hall in tears, and spent much of her allowance on inexpensive restaurant meals for several months afterward in order to avoid the scene of her humiliation.

Classmates remember her as a tall girl with a strong New England accent, who talked too quickly in a nervous, high-pitched voice. She often wore unconventional outfits and pulled her wavy red hair into a tight, very unbecoming bun. Most of the girls at Bryn Mawr seemed more at ease—and certainly better groomed—than Kate. Hepburn later reminisced, "I was never a member of the feminine club. I never knew what other girls were talking about." She did her best to appear unconcerned that many of the other students did not like or even understand her, but she missed the warmth of her large family.

sons around her sports activities. During her teens, she expressed a desire to become a doctor like her father, although she spent more time playing tennis and golf than she did studying. Nonetheless, Kate's tutor provided her with an excellent education—in everything except how to get along with other children her age.

Hepburn's sisters Peggy (left) and Marion flank their mother in this 1936 photograph. The actress remained close to her family her entire life.

Hepburn (second from right) appears as a young man in a Bryn Mawr College play. Confiding her desire to become an actress to a school friend, she was told she was "too skinny and funny-looking."

Perhaps it was her loneliness that strengthened Katharine Hepburn's love for the theater. She took some drama courses at Bryn Mawr, eventually winning several roles in college plays. Standing on the stage and hearing the applause of an audience, the awkward yet somehow elegant teenager realized she was destined to become an actress.

Her family greeted her decision with dismay. To them, choosing to become a professional actress was frivolous, like deciding to join the circus. Her father thought it was a waste of her education, and he even accused her of simply wanting to "show off." No one expected her to persist in her crazy plan. But Katharine Hepburn was already a highly determined young woman. She was sorry that her family did not support her choice, but they were the ones who had taught her to trust her own judgment.

After her graduation from Bryn Mawr in 1928, Hepburn managed to get a letter of introduction to Edwin Knopf, the manager of a Baltimore theater production company. When Knopf refused to answer her letters and phone calls, she decided to storm his office. Once it became apparent that he could not get rid of this would-be actress as easily as he had shaken others, Knopf agreed to give Hepburn a role in a play called *The Czarina*, a comedy about 18th-century Russian empress Catherine the Great. Knopf warned the eager young woman that she would have no lines, but that there would be plenty of curtsying for her to do. "My God!" Knopf later recalled, "Did she curtsy!"

Apparently she curtsied well enough to land a minor part in another Knopf production, *The Big Pond*—this time in New York. She had achieved the goal of nearly every struggling actor: landing a job on Broadway, the center of America's theater industry. Better yet, she also became the understudy for the play's star. When the leading lady was suddenly fired, Hepburn was given her role.

In movies and novels, this situation always leads to a happy ending. The young understudy turns in a wonderful performance, and overnight she becomes a star. Unfortunately, things did not work out that way for Katharine Hepburn. Her opening night was a disaster. She had a terrible case of stage fright and arrived at the theater very late. She mixed up her lines, tripped over her own feet, and talked faster and faster as her nervousness increased. By the end of the play, even the other actors could not understand what she was saying. She was fired as soon as the curtain went down.

Shortly after this fiasco, Hepburn surprised everyone by getting married. Her groom was Ludlow Ogden Smith, a handsome Philadelphia socialite who was an old friend of the Hepburn fam-

This 1934 painting depicts an elegant Hepburn and her husband, Ludlow Ogden Smith. The couple divorced that same year following a separation that began almost as soon as they married.

ily. The wedding took place on December 12, 1928, in a private ceremony at the Hepburns' home. The couple had a brief honeymoon in Bermuda before they returned to New York to live in a sparsely furnished, tiny two-room apartment.

Katharine Hepburn began to regret her impulsive act almost immediately. Nothing about married life appealed to her. She hated her new name, Kate Smith, which also happened to be the name of a sentimental popular singer. In fact, she insisted that her husband call himself Ogden Ludlow, so that she would become Mrs. Ludlow instead of Mrs. Smith. She also had no interest in homemaking. Most of all, she hated giving up her freedom. She was bored by her new life, which often consisted of hanging around the tiny apartment listening to classical music. Hepburn longed to return to acting and did little to hide her dissatisfaction from her new husband. "I behaved very badly," she later commented. "I was not fit to be married, because I thought only about myself." The newlyweds were so miserable that they separated quickly, just three weeks after the wedding. But

Hepburn's unusual blend of wholesomeness and sophistication won her many roles during her early stage career. Her problem was keeping parts: She later recalled that she was nervous, overenthusiastic, and just "couldn't act."

they continued to be friends, and there was no bitterness about the breakup. Hepburn's friend and biographer, Garson Kanin, later remarked that she and her estranged husband behaved like two people who were once in a bad accident together but managed to survive. They did not bother to get a divorce until several years later, when "Luddy" wanted to remarry, which he did with Hepburn's blessing.

After the separation, Katharine Hepburn threw herself back into her acting career. For nearly four years, she struggled to establish herself in the theater, pounding the pavement, enduring endless rounds of auditions, weathering rejection after harsh rejection. She thought her luck had finally changed when she was offered a role in *The Animal Kingdom*, a new play written by the famous Philip Barry. The star and coproducer of the play was Leslie Howard (who would later portray Ashley Wilkes in the film version of *Gone with the Wind*). Unfortunately, after a week of rehearsals, Howard told Hepburn that she had far too many distracting mannerisms, and he fired her. When she called Philip Barry to protest heatedly, he shot back, "Nobody who has your disposition could ever play light comedy! I'm glad they fired you!"

For all her bad luck—and, occasionally, bad temper—the young Katharine Hepburn had undeniable star quality. Her unusual aristocratic looks, athletic grace, and strong stage presence persuaded directors to keep offering her parts. But in those days she was not a good actress. She was too artificial, too extreme. When she was nervous, her voice became high and tinny. And she was always nervous!

Years later, Hepburn talked with biographer Charles Higham about her early struggles. "I could read a part without knowing what I was doing better than anyone in the whole world," she recalled. "I could laugh and cry, and I could always get a part quickly— but I couldn't keep it! I would lose my voice, fall down on lines, get red in the face, talk too fast, and I couldn't act. The sight of people out there just petrified me."

Most people in her shoes would have been discouraged, but Katharine Hepburn kept trying. Then, at last, she got a break. She was cast as the female lead in *The Warrior's Husband*, which opened on Broadway on March 11, 1932. Hepburn played Antiope, the queen of the Amazons, who ruled a country where women did the fighting and hunting. The sex role reversal called for in the plot was unusual, but, true to the era's conventions, Hepburn's character was tamed by a "real man" by the play's end.

The part was almost custom-made for Hepburn. In her first appearance on stage, she had to leap down a flight of stairs carrying a very heavy stuffed

Leslie Howard used a variety of tricks to disguise the fact that Hepburn, his costar in The Animal Kingdom, *was taller than he was. Some suspected that this—not her amateurish acting—was the reason behind her dismissal from the 1931 play.*

Hepburn cuts an impressive figure in The Warrior's Husband, *her first stage triumph. The athletic actress was ideally suited to her 1932 role as queen of the Amazons.*

deer. Instantly, her athletic grace and powerful presence created a sensation. The production's stage manager, Phyllis Seaton, later described Hepburn's remarkable entrance, "The audience was *amazed* by Kate. Her beauty shone through her face. Her skin was transparent, alight with color and health. Her red hair blazed around her face. . . . She *jumped* at the audience. The audience responded to her immediately. This was a star! You could smell it, you could feel it! It was all around you—the perfume of success!"

Katharine Hepburn's apprehensions about working in Hollywood proved to be well founded when RKO Studios forced her to adopt a glamorous image that was far from her natural style.

THREE

Hepburn Goes to Hollywood

By the age of 22 Katharine Hepburn thought she had already achieved the height of success. Her starring role in *The Warrior's Husband* had brought her both public and critical acclaim. She was earning nearly $75 a week—a lot of money in the 1930s, the height of the Great Depression, when the average person was lucky to make $10 a week. She had won everything for which she had been struggling.

But a new challenge soon beckoned. In the 1930s, every major film studio made hundreds of movies annually. They were always scouting for new talent, and Broadway was one of the places they often looked. The head of RKO Studios, David O. Selznick, heard about the vibrant leading lady of *The Warrior's Husband*. He thought she might be able to bring her star quality to the movie screen.

True to form, when Katharine Hepburn learned that RKO was interested in her, she was deliberately aloof. Besides, she had absorbed the typical theater actor's disdain for Hollywood, considering film to be a rather "lowbrow" medium. By this time she had an agent, Leland Hayward. She told Hayward she would accept nothing less than $1,500 a week—fully 20 times her theater salary—to go to California. She assumed that would be the last she would hear from RKO. But David O. Selznick agreed to her price if she did well on her screen test (a short scene she would play in front of the cameras to see how she looked on film).

The movie Selznick was casting was

35

Acclaimed director George Cukor was impressed by Hepburn's screen test, despite her awkwardness. He directed many of her best films, including her first, 1932's A Bill of Divorcement.

called *A Bill of Divorcement*, which would star one of the most respected actors of the time, John Barrymore. Many actresses had competed for the role of the Barrymore character's daughter, but so far the studio heads remained unimpressed. Hepburn figured that RKO's executives were probably bored with the scene used for the screen test because they had already seen it so many times. To set herself apart from the other actresses who had unsuccessfully auditioned for the role,

Hepburn asked to be allowed to use a different scene. Moreover, she got an actor friend to appear with her—with his back to the camera the whole time. "I didn't want that nonsense about the one helping with the test getting the job," she laughingly explained later.

Despite all her planning, Hepburn was quite nervous during her first screen test. When she saw it again many years later, she commented, "It was obviously the test of someone who was totally panicked. It was heartbreaking in its eagerness to please." Nor was the film's director, George Cukor, bowled over by the gangling, rather frantic actress he and David O. Selznick saw in the test. However, Cukor did perceive that Hepburn had a certain power. As he later recalled, "There was an *enormous* feeling, a *weight* about the manner in which she picked up [a] glass. I thought she was very talented in that action. David Selznick agreed. We hired her."

So, on July 1, 1932, Katharine Hepburn boarded a train in New York to make the four-day trip to California. She had persuaded her friend, American Express heiress Laura Harding, to go along with her. Hepburn embarked on this adventure wearing an oversized pants suit and a pancake hat that she considered quite chic, although her outfit must have looked odd to most observers. The journey went well until the last day, when Hepburn, standing

Hepburn plays a dramatic scene with costar David Manners in A Bill of Divorcement. *The young actress's screen debut was hailed as "exceptionally fine."*

on the observation deck, got a cinder in her eye. Soon both her eyes grew painful and—worse—hopelessly puffy and red. The studio executives waiting at the Pasadena, California, station to pick up their latest discovery were dismayed when they saw a bedraggled redhead with bloodshot eyes and an odd-looking hat step off the train that Independence Day. "My God," one of them remarked, "is this what we're sticking David [Selznick] fifteen hundred a week for?"

Just five days after her arrival in Hollywood, Hepburn started work on her first movie. She knew little about acting and absolutely nothing about appearing in front of a camera. But she had the good luck to work with veterans. Director George Cukor was especially helpful. Part of his genius was his willingness to work persistently with his stars until he had developed their strengths and diminished their weaknesses. Under his guidance, Katharine Hepburn blossomed.

John Barrymore was also generous to the newcomer. When he first met his costar, Hepburn's eyes were still inflamed, and he refused to believe her story about the cinder. "That's what they all say, my dear," he told her. After he gave her a phial of eye drops formulated to hide the effects of too much drinking, he confided, "I also hit the bottle occasionally, my dear." Hepburn later remarked that screen veteran Barrymore "just shoved me into what I ought to do before the camera. He taught me all that he could pour into one greenhorn in that short time."

In retrospect, it is apparent that Katharine Hepburn was often unsure of her craft during the filming of *A Bill of Divorcement*. There are scenes in which her emotions seem forced, her voice high and shrill; even her movements are awkward. But there are also moments when she lights up the screen. Clearly, RKO had discovered an intriguing new actress.

Years later, George Cukor said, "I'll never forget the preview. The audience had never seen a girl like that—she seemed to *bark* at them. She didn't play for sympathy at all. At first, the audience wasn't quite sure whether it liked her or not." But finally, he remembered, there came a scene in which the audience "could see she moved beautifully, and it was at that point she became a great personality, the beginnings of a star, a major Movie Queen."

A Bill of Divorcement was released in September 1932. Moderately successful at the box office, it proved a major coup for young Katharine Hepburn, whose performance was hailed in the *New York Times* as "one of the finest characterizations seen on the screen." Suddenly everyone was curious about her. She was besieged by photographers and interviewers from newspapers and magazines. Overwhelmed by all the attention, Hepburn refused to talk to the press or, alternatively, baited reporters by telling outrageous lies—strategies that only served to stoke the fires of public curiosity. RKO, for its part, kept the gossip mills churning by spreading false rumors that she was a descendant of Mary, Queen of Scots, and a multimillion-dollar heiress. And they immediately cast her in another film.

Her second movie was a 1933 melodrama called *Christopher Strong*. Hepburn played an airplane pilot who falls in love with a married man. She eagerly plunged into the role, reading about female aviators such as Amelia Earhart and Amy Johnson. Hepburn cut a wonderfully romantic figure in her pilot's costume, which consisted of trousers, a leather jacket, and a long

Hepburn mans the cockpit in her second film, Christopher Strong, *a 1933 tearjerker in which she played a strong-willed aviator who meets a tragic end.*

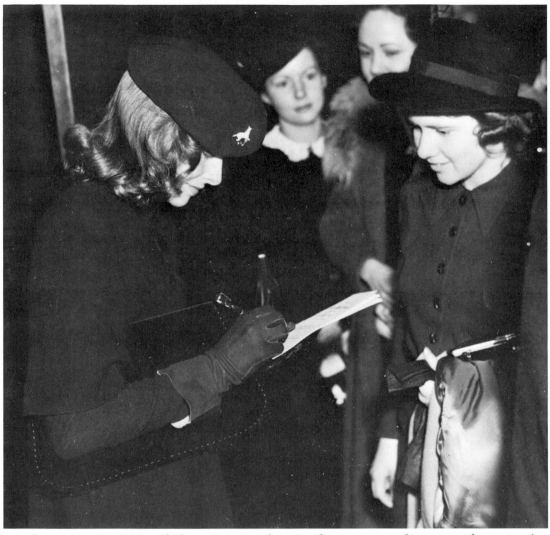

Hepburn signs an autograph for a stagestruck young fan, a rare act for a star who was quite uncomfortable with public adulation—especially when it infringed on her private life.

silk scarf. Unfortunately, the script was uninspired, and the public did not take to *Christopher Strong*. But Hepburn won some favorable reviews for her performance. One critic wrote, "That troubled, masque-like face, the high, strident, raucous, rasping voice, the straight, broad-shouldered boyish figure—perhaps they may all grate on you, but they compel attention, and they fascinate an audience."

Just six months after her arrival in Hollywood, she was already at work on her third movie, *Morning Glory*, the story of a young understudy who becomes a star. The plot was already stale in 1933, but her strong performance captivated the audience. The role also brought her one of Hollywood's highest honors—an Academy Award nomination.

Hepburn considered it a great achievement merely to have been nominated, especially at that early stage of her career. She was so sure she would not win that she decided to take a trip to Europe rather than stay in the United States to attend the ceremonies. She was utterly amazed when a reporter tracked her down in Paris and told her the Best Actress Oscar was hers.

Already well established as a Hollywood eccentric, Hepburn also showed herself to be a maverick in her romantic life during the filming of *Morning Glory*. After she reluctantly agreed to a date with her handsome costar, Douglas Fairbanks, Jr., Hepburn complained of a headache and asked the sought-after movie idol to take her home early. "So I dropped her home," Fairbanks recalls. "After doing so I just pulled up at the roadside. I don't know why. Maybe just to moon—to think, 'Oh, dear me—isn't she grand?' And the next thing I saw out of the corner of my eye, at the back of the house, running through to another street was the little figure of Kate dashing out—and going off somewhere into someone else's car." Brushing off important leading men such as Fairbanks was certainly not something an ordinary young actress would have done—but it was becoming increasingly clear that

Katharine Hepburn was hardly just an ordinary young actress.

In 1933, she portrayed the tomboyish Jo in a film version of *Little Women*, the beloved novel by Louisa May Alcott. George Cukor, who had directed Hepburn's screen debut, headed up this movie as well. He tried to avoid sentimentality and to follow Alcott's realistic story about a family of women left alone while the only man in the house fights in the Civil War. After its release, the movie became one of the top 10 money-makers of the year. Costumes and sets were authentic, and both were nominated for Academy Awards, as were Cukor and the picture itself. Hepburn did not receive a nomination, probably because she had just won an Oscar the previous year. But Cukor gave her much of the credit for the movie's success. "She was born for the part of Jo," he told an interviewer. "She's tender and odd and funny, sweet and yet tough, intensely loyal, with an enormous sense of family and all of Jo's burning ambition and at heart a pure, clean simplicity and firmness."

Cukor was right when he said that Hepburn was devoted to her family. The young actress stayed in constant touch with her parents and siblings, although they were more than 3,000 miles apart. During their many long-distance phone conversations, the emphasis was usually on the Hepburn family's adventures in the East, not on

Douglas Fairbanks, Jr., stares deep into Hepburn's eyes in 1933's Morning Glory. *The film won Hepburn her first Academy Award—and the admiration of her costar, who later confessed to having "a particularly big crush on her."*

Kate's supposedly glamorous life in Hollywood. As she told a biographer, "Father and Mother never came to Hollywood. They were not remotely interested in picture-making, and why should they be? Their own life was far too interesting, and far removed from the drudgery of Hollywood."

Hepburn made a point of avoiding the parties at which young actresses were expected to attract newspaper columnists and to meet the "right people"—those who could help them with their careers. Instead, after a day on the movie set, she would come home around six, scrub off her screen makeup, and have dinner in bed while reviewing the next day's script. She was asleep most nights by 10 o'clock. Hepburn also kept up the pastimes she had enjoyed in Hartford. On her days off she usually golfed, played tennis, or hiked in the California hills. Wholesome and independent, Hepburn was certainly a Hollywood original, and her originality fascinated the movie-going public.

No one could have maintained such a winning streak forever: a hit play and four movies—one an Oscar winner, another a film classic—all in roughly one year. In 1933, Hepburn's career began a downhill slide that would last until 1938. Part of the problem was the roles she was cast in, both on Broadway and at RKO. Following an unsuccessful six-week Broadway run in a sentimental drama called *The Lake*, Hepburn was

Famous for preferring slacks to skirts, Katharine Hepburn was somehow coaxed into displaying her legs for this early publicity photograph.

Hepburn is treated for injuries during the filming of Sylvia Scarlett. *When Cary Grant refused to brave the Pacific surf, George Cukor (standing, right) revised the scene and sent Hepburn to save half-drowned actress Natalie Paley.*

cast as a hillbilly in a 1934 movie titled *Spitfire*. Producer Pandro Berman later remembered this part as a one disastrously inappropriate for the sophisticated Bryn Mawr graduate. "What a mistake that was! Here was this cultured New England lady playing a gypsy squatter.... but Kate seemed to love it." In 1935 she appeared in *Break*

of Hearts, the story of a young girl infatuated with an alcoholic orchestra conductor old enough to be her father. Another box office failure was *A Woman Rebels*, a 1936 film about a suffragist. The script was mediocre, but Hepburn wanted to make the film, partly in recognition of her mother's struggle to win the vote for women.

Katharine Hepburn (right) won the hearts of audiences as the irrepressible tomboy Jo March in a 1933 film version of Little Women.

The only successes Hepburn had in these years were 1935's *Alice Adams*, which won her a second Academy Award nomination, and 1937's *Stage Door*, in which she shared star billing with Ginger Rogers.

RKO began to worry about the future of its young star. Studio executives had cast her in these melodramatic parts because they had pegged her as a "serious" actress. As Pandro Berman later said of this period, "By this time I realized Kate wasn't a movie star. She wasn't going to become one either, in the sense that Joan Crawford or Marlene Dietrich were—actresses able to drag an audience in by their own efforts. She was a hit only in hit pictures.

She couldn't save a flop."

Hepburn certainly did not look like other movie stars. Her face was bony, with strong features, and her figure was wiry rather than full. Her bright red hair was uncontrollable, and her gray-green eyes were sometimes disconcertingly direct in their gaze. Photographer and designer Cecil Beaton rather unflatteringly described Hepburn as a woman who "has a face that belongs to the sea and the wind, with large rocking-horse nostrils and teeth that you just know bite an apple every day." Referring to her thin figure, another contemporary quipped, "You could throw a hat at her, and wherever it hit, it would stick."

Moreover, Hepburn refused to behave like other Hollywood celebrities.

Movie siren Marlene Dietrich strikes a vampish pose in this scene from the 1936 film Desire. *The sultry actress was a big box-office draw during the period in which Hepburn's career was floundering.*

Whenever she reluctantly agreed to attend a party, she insisted on wearing her trademark man-tailored slacks with a plain dark sweater, rather than a lavish gown. She still frequently wore her hair pulled straight back in a severe, unfashionable bun. And while other young actresses would giggle and smile and let famous older men do all the talking, Hepburn's high-pitched voice would pierce the room, trumpeting her own strong opinions. As she spoke, she always held her chin high, as if daring her listeners to disagree with her.

Soon RKO's executives concluded that Hepburn was just too forceful to gain public acceptance as a film heroine. She lacked the traditional "feminine" appeal—young, voluptuous, and naive—of the "Sweater Girls," the ideal of the 1930s. Therefore, the studio determined it would change her image, in the hope of saving her career.

Many of the publicity photos of Katharine Hepburn in the 1930s illustrate RKO's strategy. Her strong angular features were softened by a mass of fluffy curls around her face, or hidden by romantic wide-brimmed hats. Her narrow lips were painted over with lipstick to make them look pouty and full. Her flamboyant red hair was toned down to a deep, more acceptable auburn, and her freckles were camouflaged with thick layers of pancake makeup and powder.

With her "improved" looks, Hepburn was now cast in "sweet" roles. She played nice, old-fashioned, submissive women who sacrificed everything for the men they loved. In *The Little Minister* (1934), she portrayed a rebellious young woman who renounces her "evil" past and decides that salvation lies in getting a husband. "He must rule me," her character announces; "He must be my master." In 1937's *Quality Street*, she played a desperate spinster who pretends to be someone else in order to attract a suitor. She also appeared in a rash of "costume dramas" (historical romances) that concealed her athletic grace in Victorian hoop skirts and crinolines. The characters she portrayed had aristocratic-sounding names such as Lady Babbie, Pamela Thistlewaite, and Phoebe Throssel.

But the campaign to tame Katharine Hepburn was a failure, thanks to her own strong personality. All the studio executives did was destroy her natural appeal and make her look awkward and foolish on the screen. One film critic, Frank Nugent, panned her performance in *Quality Street*, saying, "Her Phoebe Throssel needs a neurologist far more than a husband. Such flutterings and jitterings and twitchings, such hand-wringings and mouth-quaverings, such runnings about and eyebrow-raisings have not been seen on the screen in many a moon." A review of her 1936 performance in *Mary of Scotland* complained, "Katharine Hepburn acts like a Bryn Mawr senior in a

Looking like "one of the boys," Hepburn meets with fellow golfers before a charity tournament. Her tailored clothes were considered outrageous during her early career, but she has since been acknowledged as a fashion trendsetter.

May Day pageant." For the most part, movie audiences were equally unimpressed, and it became increasingly difficult to sell tickets to movies starring Katharine Hepburn.

The worst moment came in 1938 when Harry Brandt, president of the Independent Theatre Owners of America, ran full-page ads in newspapers all over the country labeling Katharine Hepburn and a few other stars, including celebrated screen goddesses Greta Garbo and Mae West, "Box Office Poison." The ad charged that profits fell off every time theaters showed a film starring Hepburn. Brandt urged RKO to protect itself—and theater owners everywhere—by refusing to cast her in any more movies.

With the Brandt campaign, Hepburn finally lost her last toehold in Hollywood. It looked as if her movie career, begun so brilliantly just six years before, was finished.

Hepburn sweeps the floor as she portrays a "traditional" heroine. Despite the pincurls and ruffles, she was unconvincing in these roles—and branded "Box Office Poison" in 1938.

49

Katharine Hepburn's future in Hollywood was uncertain when she left California in 1938. Two years later, she returned to the film capital armed with enough popularity—and power—to dictate her own terms.

FOUR

Conquering a Crisis

Clearly it was time for Hepburn to retrench—to escape from Hollywood's pressures and false values, as well as from her own failure. So in 1938 she left California for her family's home in her beloved Connecticut. There she played tennis and golf, walked along the shore, and swam in the Atlantic Ocean. And there she began to rethink her goals and to redefine her career.

One thing she was sure of: Her future was not with RKO. She had bought out her contract earlier that year, after the studio bosses tried to push her into playing a role in a mediocre film called *Mother Carey's Chickens*. Now ·she resolved that she would never again put herself at the mercy of a studio. In the future, she would choose her roles and play dynamic women who tackled life's challenges head on. There would be no more shy and simpering hero-

ines for Katharine Hepburn. She would dress, look, and behave on the screen much more like the person she was in real life.

Hepburn knew that her decision was risky at best. The public was used to idolizing such sweetly feminine stars as Olivia de Havilland, or such outrageously sexy *femmes fatales* as Jean Harlow and Mae West. Audiences might refuse to accept a leading lady with a boyish figure, a candid stare, and a Yankee twang. Moreover, now that she had broken with RKO, she would have to find her own financial backing. And she doubted that investors would rush to put money into movies with a star who had been called "Box Office Poison."

But Katharine Hepburn was determined that if she failed again, she would fail on her own.

Mae West, famous for her suggestive humor and hourglass figure, reclines on a chaise lounge. Although she cultivated a more traditional feminine appeal, West, like Hepburn, was one of the most independent and tough-minded women in Hollywood.

Late in 1938 she got one more chance in Hollywood: She received an offer to costar with Cary Grant in *Holiday*, directed by her old friend George Cukor. Hepburn was well-suited to the female leading role—a high-spirited, mischievous woman. But the film's story line about a wealthy family alienated movie audiences, who were still suffering through the Great Depression that gripped America in the 1930s.

Undaunted, Hepburn decided she would return to the stage. The theater was her first love and the site of her first success. Theatergoers were more sophisticated than the mass screen audience, and best of all, staging a play cost much less than shooting a film. She thought it would be relatively easy to find investors to back a play if only she could find the right "vehicle"—a script with a starring role that would best display her talents. As it turned out, the vehicle she was looking for was right under her nose.

Oddly enough, Hepburn had become good friends with Philip Barry, the playwright who had been so sarcastic when Leslie Howard fired her from *The Animal Kingdom* in 1931. It was a bad start for a friendship, but each had come to recognize the other as a professional with a strong commitment to excellence. During a weekend visit to Connecticut, Barry told Hepburn that he was writing a play about a young Philadelphia socialite named Tracy Lord. On the surface Lord was icy, covering up her true feelings in a quest for perfection that left her bitter and unhappy. In the course of the play, she would learn to judge others more realistically, to temper her tough standards with compassion. The changes Hepburn herself had undergone since her days as a rather willful novice actress had partly inspired the character of Barry's heroine.

Cary Grant was Hepburn's costar in Holiday, *made after her 1938 break with RKO Pictures. The film was a critical success, but it failed to revive Hepburn's flagging career.*

Barry was convinced that only Katharine Hepburn was suited to play his haughty yet appealing heroine. He knew it would take a special actress to show how Lord changed, finally acquiring "an understanding heart" by the end of the play. As Hepburn listened to her friend sketch out the plot, she knew she could play the role. It would be a perfect vehicle for her return to Broadway.

While Philip Barry drafted the script,

to be called *The Philadelphia Story*, Hepburn tried to raise the funds to stage the play on Broadway. Unfortunately, most experienced producers were doubtful that a play starring Katharine Hepburn would sell tickets. Her financial difficulties were compounded because Philip Barry's recent plays had an uneven record at the box office. Finally, the Theater Guild, a group of Broadway writers and stars that Hepburn had worked with in the past, expressed interest in the project, but because the group had just backed several unsuccessful plays, it had very little money.

Hepburn refused to admit defeat. When she learned that the Theater Guild could raise only a quarter of the capital needed, she immediately put up another 25 percent out of her own pocket. Then she talked Philip Barry into doing the same. The remaining 25 percent came from a man Hepburn was dating at the time, the wildly eccentric billionaire industrialist Howard Hughes. It was Hughes who, in turn, persuaded Hepburn to buy the film rights to *The Philadelphia Story*. Not only would the movie rights be very valuable if the play proved a success, they would also give her great control over the film production. She believed in the play so much that she even gave up her salary, taking only a modest percentage of the profits for her performance. Hepburn was risking everything—but during the play's pre-

Hepburn's career doldrums ended in 1939 when she appeared with Joseph Cotten (left) and Van Heflin in The Philadelphia Story. *Writer Philip Barry created the play's spirited heroine with Hepburn in mind.*

James Stewart (left), Cary Grant (center), and Katharine Hepburn are frozen by an invading photographer's camera in the final moment of the film version of The Philadelphia Story.

Broadway road tour, her faith was re-warded with successes in such cities as Washington, D.C., and New Haven, Connecticut. Nonetheless, when the play opened in New York on March 28, 1939, she was so nervous she feared she would not be able to walk out on stage. As curtain time approached, she struggled to conquer her stage fright by mumbling over and over to herself, "This is Indianapolis, this is Indianapolis."

But her fears were unfounded, to say the least. *The Philadelphia Story* was a rousing, triumphant hit. New York's critics loved it, and the public thronged to buy tickets. The play ran on Broad-way for months, and then in the fall of 1940, Hepburn took it out on a national tour. *The Philadelphia Story* eventually reaped more than $1.5 million, far out-stripping its backers' wildest hopes. On the night of the last performance, Hep-burn told the audience, "The curtain will never be rung down on this play," and strode off the brightly lit stage in triumph. Her successful gamble even began to silence the talk in Hollywood that she was a box office jinx. As one critic cautiously wrote, "All may be for-given and forgotten."

Indeed, the movie bosses who had so recently spurned Hepburn now be-gan to court her avidly, hoping for the chance to film *The Philadelphia Story*. Because she owned the movie rights, Hepburn could now deal with them as

Billionaire industrialist Howard Hughes prepares his plane for takeoff. Hepburn wisely took Hughes's advice and bought the film rights to The Philadelphia Story.

an equal—or perhaps as a superior. Sporting the high-heeled platform shoes that some people claimed she wore to look more intimidating, Hep-burn met the Hollywood bosses head on. She finally signed a deal with

Hepburn's mischievous Tracy Lord leaves suitors (left to right) Cary Grant, James Stewart, and John Howard looking puzzled in this publicity photo for The Philadelphia Story.

Metro-Goldwyn-Mayer (MGM) for the handsome sum of $250,000, with the stipulation that her favorite director, George Cukor, work on the film.

Shooting got under way in 1940. Hepburn, of course, starred as Tracy Lord. Cary Grant was cast as her former husband, who wins her once more in the end. And Jimmy Stewart played the brash, young reporter who encourages Lord to get drunk and go for a midnight skinny-dip.

When *The Philadelphia Story* hit the movie theaters late in 1940, Hepburn scored another bonanza. Not only was it one of the top 10 money-making movies of that year, it remains a much-loved classic today. Its opening scene is one of the most memorable in cinematic history: The door to a posh mansion opens, and Hepburn pitches out a set of golf clubs after the departing Grant. When he tries to appeal to her sympathy, she pulls a club out of the bag, breaks it over her knee, and flings the pieces after him. Finally, even the courtly Grant has had enough. He walks back to the door, puts his hand over her face, and flattens her with a firm shove backward.

Hepburn won her third Academy Award nomination for *The Philadelphia Story*, although Ginger Rogers would ultimately win the award that year. But even more important than the Oscar nomination was the lesson the experience taught Hepburn: At a time when few stars and even fewer women could escape the grip of the studios, she discovered she could stand up to powerful movie executives—and win.

Hollywood's most prestigious studio, MGM, offered her a lucrative long-term contract that gave her the choice of leading man and director, story ap-

Hepburn and British novelist Hugh Walpole relax at the home of George Cukor, director of The Philadelphia Story.

proval, and time off for stage work. Katharine Hepburn was back in business. She had risen from failure to become a spectacular success. Hepburn had kept her faith in herself, in her talent, in her integrity—and she had won on her own terms.

Hepburn and Spencer Tracy tie the knot in this scene from their first movie together, 1942's Woman of the Year. *The actors began a 25-year romance during the film's shooting.*

FIVE

Enter Spencer Tracy

Naturally, now Katharine Hepburn wanted to find a project of equal merit to crown her triumph in *The Philadelphia Story*. Then, as today, it was hard to find scripts featuring powerful, intelligent heroines, but Hepburn finally chose one coauthored by Ring Lardner, Jr., the son of the famous short story writer. *Woman of the Year* told the story of an unlikely romance between Tess Harding, a high-powered political columnist, and Sam Craig, a tough sportswriter for the same newspaper. They fall in love and marry, but they do not live happily ever after. Harding is much too busy with her career to be the wife Craig wants. Eventually, he decides to leave—on the very same night she receives an award as Woman of the Year. By the film's end, the two main characters have reunited,

but their future together still seems uncertain.

Like the heroine of *The Philadelphia Story*, Tess Harding is a strong, confident character who comes to recognize her own human failings. Hepburn was obviously perfect for the part. But who could play the hard-boiled writer who would match her in drive and grit? After a great deal of searching, Hepburn finally chose Spencer Tracy. He had won acclaim as the gruff but lovable hero of such popular films as *San Francisco, Captains Courageous*, and *Boys' Town*. Although Hepburn had never worked with him, before, she believed he would be able to project a strength on screen that would complement her own.

Hepburn appeared on the set for the first day's shooting wearing her formidable platform heels, with her hair piled high on her head to make herself look even more imposing. "I fear I may be a little too tall for you, Mr. Tracy," she said on meeting her 5 foot 10 inch costar. Producer Joseph Mankiewicz, who already knew both actors, told Hepburn, "Don't worry, he'll cut you down to size." A romantically charged sense of rivalry characterized Tracy and Hepburn's personal relationship—and their films together—from the very start.

On the set, everyone noticed the special chemistry that seemed to exist between the two stars. As they competed, they also spurred each other on to stronger, more vivid performances. Years later, Hepburn reminisced with television journalist Barbara Walters about the way she and Tracy had worked together in *Woman of the Year*. "We had a scene in a restaurant where I reached forward, and I knocked over a glass of water by mistake; I was that excited playing with him, because I admired him so much." She continued, "He looked at the glass of water that was turned over and took out his handkerchief and handed it to me. So I thought, the old son-of-a-gun, he's not going to get away with that. So I began to mop it up." She laughed, "And then I got down under the table and I continued mopping and playing the scene."

As the filming of *Woman of the Year* progressed, the sense of challenge between Hepburn and Tracy turned to warmer feelings. Producer Joe Mankiewicz recalled, "One knew towards the end of the film that they were cozy with each other, and when they had to come back and shoot a new ending, it was quite obvious that they were in love."

It was the start of a legendary romance, clouded by one major obstacle: Tracy was already married. He and Louise Tracy had drifted apart before he met Hepburn, and they were no longer living in the same house. But Louise was the mother of his two children, and Tracy respected her. Moreover, he was a devout Catholic for whom divorce was unthinkable.

Some of Hepburn's friends speculated that perhaps she had fallen for Tracy simply *because* he was not free to marry her. Her previous attempt at marriage had been a spectacular failure, and Katharine Hepburn did not like to fail at anything. Besides, she was pessimistic about marriage for anyone in her profession. "An actor should never marry," she said in an interview, "not even another actor. You're too involved with yourself, and your work is too demanding, to give the necessary amount of attention to another human being. Inevitably, that person feels left out. And becomes unhappy."

Woman of the Year *launched one of the most successful movie teams in history. Hepburn later attributed their popularity to the fact that she and Tracy "balanced each other's natures."*

Spencer Tracy married Louise Treadwell in 1923. Although the couple had lived apart for years before Tracy fell in love with Hepburn, the devoutly Catholic Tracy never divorced his wife.

So Hepburn and Tracy invented a different kind of love affair that remained, nonetheless, deep and committed for more than 25 years. French actress Simone Signoret, who worked on a movie with Hepburn in the early 1960s, told a magazine reporter that the star disappeared from the set every day promptly at 4:30 P.M. so she could shop for and cook Spencer Tracy's din-

Director Frank Capra admiringly noted that when Hepburn and Tracy played a scene together, "Cameras, lights, microphones, and written scripts ceased to exist. And the director did just what the crews and other actors did—sat, watched, and marveled."

ner. Signoret said Hepburn acted "like a schoolgirl in love"—all the more remarkable because at that time Hepburn had known Tracy for 20 years.

Out of respect for Louise Tracy, they

kept their relationship a secret. The two actors rarely appeared together in public, and when they did, they were always part of a group. They did not travel together, and if they both happened to be on location for a film, they did not even stay in the same hotel. Close friends knew about their romance, of course, but they, too, helped to keep the secret.

Part of the glue that held Katharine Hepburn and Spencer Tracy together for so many years was their professional teamwork. Tracy was known for his ease and naturalism on the screen. He once told an interviewer that the secret of acting was simply, "Learn your lines and don't bump into the furniture." He taught Hepburn how to relax in front of the camera, helping her curb the overacting that marred some of her early films. In return, Hepburn acted as a quick-witted foil, soft-pedaling Tracy's terse gruffness. Their union was hardly placid, because as two strong individuals, they often butted heads—a dynamic that was mirrored in the characters they played. But together they were undeniably electric, perfectly balanced partners, both on camera and off.

The combination worked magic at the box office, too, beginning with their first collaboration: *Woman of the Year* brought Hepburn to a new peak of popularity, winning her a fourth Oscar nomination. Of the nine films Hepburn and Tracy would make together, several have proved enduring favorites. One such classic is *Adam's Rib* (1949), written for them by Garson Kanin and his wife, actress Ruth Gordon. The script cast Hepburn and Tracy as law-yers married to each other who are defending opposite sides in a court case. Before long, the fight in the courtroom spills over into their private life; and it seems that when the trial ends, their marriage will, too. But as in many Hepburn-Tracy films, the plot ends happily—once the wife admits she has gone too far. As Hepburn described the characters she and Tracy portrayed: "The woman is very quick, on to everything, ready to go forward with anything, emotional. The man is slower, more solid, very funny at times, good with quips, ultimately subduing the woman, thereby making her happy because she really wants to be subdued, or at least to let him think she's subdued."

Nowadays, Hepburn's words sound strange, surprisingly submissive—especially coming from a woman who has symbolized feminine strength—but they must be considered in the context of their time. In the late 1940s, women had been voting for fewer than thirty years and were openly discriminated against; that they could deal with men on truly equal terms was nearly inconceivable. Hepburn was creating characters on stage and screen who *were* bold and assertive—to the extent that most people could accept or even imagine, given the era's social stereotypes.

Other famous Hepburn-Tracy films include *Pat and Mike* and *Desk Set*. The former was a 1952 comedy depicting

Tracy and Hepburn square off across their law books in this publicity photograph for Adam's Rib. *Even off camera, a loving rivalry characterized the actors' relationship.*

Garson Kanin and his wife, actress Ruth Gordon, wrote the screenplays for such popular Hepburn-Tracy vehicles as Adam's Rib *and* Pat and Mike.

An avid sportswoman, Hepburn polishes her tennis game for her role as a professional athlete in the 1952 comedy Pat and Mike.

the clash between an athlete (Hepburn) and her tough-talking manager (Tracy). Of course, by the end of the film, the characters have fallen in love. In 1957's *Desk Set*, Hepburn plays a research librarian tangling with Tracy, a hard-nosed efficiency expert. Hepburn turned in a magnificent performance as the librarian fighting to avoid being replaced with a computer. As one critic remarked, "Miss Hepburn obviously is a woman who is superior to a thinking machine."

Along with their joint productions, both actors continued to pursue their independent careers. Hepburn made 19 films during her years with Spencer Tracy—more than half of them on her own. From 1942, the year they first met, until Tracy's death in 1967, Katharine Hepburn enjoyed the most feverish — and happiest—period of her life.

By the 1950s Katharine Hepburn had unquestionably attained stardom. Her fame enabled her to work with many of the world's finest actors and directors.

SIX

Life at the Top

By the early 1950s, Katharine Hepburn was at the height of her profession. She was internationally known as a seasoned dramatic actress with an equal flair for comedy—and as a rock-solid box office draw. Still, she had not lost the drive for perfection that had marked her early career. As producer Pandro Berman recalled her RKO days, "She was difficult—but even when she drove you mad, you had to admire her spunk, her guts. She got exactly what she wanted—wouldn't work any later than she thought she should, wanted triple overtime—but when she was on the set, she toiled like a bridgemender." Another RKO producer, Larry

Weingarten, added, "People always said to me, 'She's trying to do everything.' And my reply was, 'The thing I'm afraid of is that she *can* do everything!' Producer, director, cameraman! That's what she was!"

With time, her intensity had mellowed, but she remained a consummate professional, deeply committed to her art. As actor Robert Morley, who worked with her in 1951, remembered, "She was the sort of lady who, when you were doing a scene with her and you weren't very clever about getting into the right position or were about to fall over one of the cables, would continue with her performance, impeccably, and at the same time manage to push you into the right place with a friendly shove—and pick up the cable as well!"

That professionalism would be rigorously tested during the shooting of *The African Queen*, her first Technicolor movie, in 1951. Hepburn played Rose Sayer, a prim missionary who convinces a hard-drinking riverboat captain, Charlie Allnut (Humphrey Bogart), to destroy a German gunboat in World War I Africa. Director John Huston decided to shoot on location to make the film more authentic. And authentic it was—there were crocodiles in the river and poisonous snakes in the portable toilets. The cast suffered a series of catastrophes, including a rash of tropical diseases and an attack of stinging red ants so vicious that Huston was forced to temporarily halt the filming.

The hardships of location shooting sealed the friendship between Hepburn and her costar, Humphrey Bogart. Although she scolded both Bogart and Huston for their drinking and off-color banter, she soon came to be accepted as "one of the boys." One reason for this acceptance was her

Hepburn and Humphrey Bogart struggle through the jungle in a scene from the 1951 movie The African Queen. *Undaunted by the rigors of location shooting, Hepburn inspired awe among her fellow cast members, including the rugged Bogart.*

unflagging enthusiasm. Bogart's rec-
ollections of Hepburn in Africa were
tinged with both awe and humor:

> You get a load of the babe stalking
> through an African jungle as though she
> had beaten [explorer David] Livingstone
> to it. Her shirttail is carefully torn for
> casual effect and is flapping out of her
> jeans. She pounces on the flora and
> fauna with a home movie camera like a
> kid going to his first Christmas tree, and
> she blunders within ten feet of a wild
> boar's tusks for a close-up of the beast.
> About every other minute she wrings
> her hands in ecstasy and says, "What
> divine natives! What divine morning-
> glories!" Brother, your brow goes up
> . . .Is this something from *The
> Philadelphia Story?*

Hepburn, in turn, would later say of
the rough-hewn Bogart, "He was one
of the few men I've known who was
proud of being an actor. . . . He watched
out for me, like a father, when we made
The African Queen. A total gentleman."

The African Queen proved a triumph,
both artistically and financially, winning four Academy Award nominations: for best actor, best actress
(Hepburn's fifth), best director, and
best screenplay. It brought Bogart the
only Oscar of his career, and although
Hepburn lost to Vivien Leigh for *A
Streetcar Named Desire*, many con-
sider her powerful characterization of
Rose Sayer, the stiff prude who is trans-
formed into a valiant heroine, to be one
of her finest screen performances. *The
African Queen* remains one of the most
loved and revered classics in movie
history.

Hepburn followed *The African
Queen* with her seventh film with Spencer Tracy, *Pat and Mike* (1952). She was
then offered the chance to return to
the stage—this time in London, the
home of some of the world's most celebrated theatrical productions. She
made her London debut not in an
American play but, surprisingly for an
actress with a decided Yankee twang,
in *The Millionairess*, by the great Irish
dramatist George Bernard Shaw. It was
the first time the play, written in 1935,
had ever been staged in a major theater—apparently for good reason, as it
was savaged by the critics. But Hepburn's performance dazzled the sophisticated London audience. "No one
else that I can remember," one reviewer remarked, "by sheer personal
vitality has bludgeoned her way to
success."

After bringing *The Millionairess* to
Broadway late in 1952, Hepburn retired
from the limelight for a while—until
the famous British director David Lean
tempted her with what has been called
"one of the greatest 'woman-oriented'
screenplays of the decade." In *Summertime* (1955), Hepburn played an
American spinster schoolteacher who
takes a vacation in Venice and falls in
love with an Italian shopkeeper—only
to discover he is married and the father
of three children.

This sympathetic drama about a
lonely older woman (Hepburn herself
was 45 at the time) featured many in-

Rejecting the idea of using a stunt double, Hepburn permanently damaged her eyes when she fell into a polluted Venetian canal for this scene from Summertime, made in 1955.

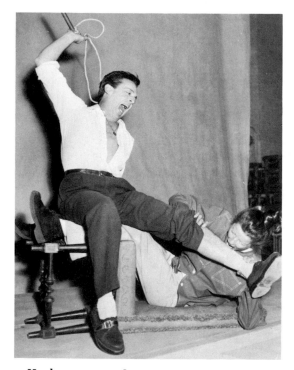

Hepburn pretends to take a bite from actor Robert Helpmann's leg as they rehearse Shakespeare's The Taming of the Shrew *before their 1955 tour of Australia.*

terludes of high comedy. In one scene, the tourist heroine becomes so engrossed in her photography that she forgets she is standing in front of a Venetian canal and falls right in.

Hepburn could have had a stunt double handle this scene, but as usual, her sense of professionalism ruled. She knew that the fall would be funnier and more convincing if she did it herself. As she later recalled:

> I knew how dirty the water was, so I took all kinds of precautions—even washed my mouth with antiseptic, put special dressing on my hair, wore shoes

that wouldn't waterlog. But like an idiot, I forgot my eyes. Well, the water was a *sewer*! Filthy, brackish, full of trash. When I got out, my eyes were running. They've been running ever since. I have the most ghastly infection—I'll never lose it until the day I die. When people ask me why I cry such a lot in pictures, I say, mysteriously, "Canal in Venice."

Summertime was another hit film for Hepburn, bringing her yet another—her sixth—Oscar nomination. One reviewer used boxing images to describe Hepburn's artistic drive: "For much of the time ... the film resolves itself into a kind of championship fight with Venice in one corner and Miss Katharine Hepburn in the other—and it says much for [cinematographer] Jack Hildyard's photography that Venice is able for so long to survive. For Venice is up against a true champion, and a champion persuaded by Mr. Lean to fight at the top of her form."

Hepburn's formidable professional image often affected her private life, and it did during the filming of *Summertime*. When the day's shooting was over, the crew—notably director David Lean and costar Rossano Brazzi—left the actress to her own devices. She later remarked, "I suppose they all thought I would have madly exciting things to do and left me to it." One night, as she was sitting by a Venetian canal "feeling lonely and neglected," she was approached by a plumber, who apparently knew nothing of Hepburn's mystique. "I was glad to talk to anyone who looked reasonably all

This Beverly Hills home, although modest by Hollywood standards, was the most lavish of the houses Hepburn rented on the West Coast.

right," she recalled, "so we went out together for a walk through Venice." Hepburn may have been imposing, but clearly she was no snob.

In 1955, Hepburn missed the magic of a live audience and decided to tour Australia with the world's most honored Shakespeare players, the Old Vic Company. Her regal bearing and sheer power onstage captivated an audience accustomed to seeing traditional Brit-

ish stars portray Katharina in *The Taming of the Shrew*, Isabella in *Measure for Measure*, and Portia in *The Merchant of Venice*.

Yet, for all her fame, Hepburn continued to live with unconventional simplicity. While other Hollywood stars were buying or building extravagant mansions, Hepburn lived in a modest, rented bungalow on George Cukor's estate. She never purchased a

Hepburn shares a laugh with poet Carl Sandburg (top) and Secretary of the Interior Harold L. Ickes at a Democratic party fund-raiser. "I'm not very political," Hepburn once said, "I just believe in being liberal and affirmative."

house on the West Coast, perhaps because she never felt fully at home there. She also continued to avoid Hollywood parties, preferring to spend evenings entertaining at home, preparing meals for friends, and engaging in spirited discussions.

In his book, *Tracy and Hepburn*, her friend Garson Kanin offered a glimpse into Hepburn's private world:

> When you enter her world you are expected to observe its strictures, and you do so without question. You eat a cooked fruit with every meat dish; you arrive on time and leave as early as possible (say on her third yawn); you do not gossip; you agree with every one of her many opinions and approve each of her numerous plans. You do not get drunk no matter how much you drink; you love her dog Lobo; you applaud the efforts or output or creation of all her friends (whether they or their works are known to you or not); you do not complain. You say nothing that may not be repeated; you refrain from lies, dissemblances and exaggerations; you omit discussion of your physical state, symptoms, or ailments; you take her advice; you do not use obscene, coarse or lewd expressions.

In her dress, too, Hepburn rejected Hollywood's love of glamour, preferring to wear casual, comfortable clothes. In *Tracy and Hepburn*, Garson Kanin recounts an amusing anecdote about a mid-1950s trip to London, England, with Tracy and Hepburn. The men stayed in the posh Claridge's Hotel, while Hepburn chose to stay in a simpler inn, although she visited her two friends often. One day the assis-tant manager of Claridge's drew Kanin and Tracy aside to discuss the "problem" of Hepburn's appearance. The hotel had dress regulations, yet Hepburn insisted on walking through the lobby in slacks. The assistant manager was scandalized. According to him, the other guests were scandalized as well. Miss Hepburn would have to conform to the dress code, or Tracy and Kanin would be asked to leave.

Tracy was very reluctant to tell Hepburn about this "problem," but he finally worked up his courage. She replied that she *couldn't* wear a dress because she did not own one. Finally, Hepburn solved the problem in her own indomitable way; she continued to wear slacks, but she entered through the rear entrance and used the freight elevator, thereby avoiding the main lobby and the scandalized eyes. Eventually she struck up friendships with the members of the hotel staff she encountered on her unusual route through the building. As she told Tracy, "They may not love me in the front of this hotel, but they *adore* me backstairs."

Hepburn stood out, during the conservative 1940s and 1950s, in many other areas as well. The prevailing feminine ideal was the suburban housewife; and so stars such as Debbie Reynolds and Doris Day were photographed in frilly aprons, waving feather dusters over knickknacks. Yet Hepburn openly proclaimed that for her, and

Actress Debbie Reynolds, shown here knitting, embodied the 1950's ideal of womanhood. Hepburn, in contrast, openly admitted that she preferred the life of a career woman to that of a homemaker.

possibly for other working women, conventional married life was all wrong. She also criticized the powerful House Un-American Affairs Committee, a group that gained influence as tensions between the United States and the Soviet Union increased following World War II. This congressional

committee was dedicated to weeding out suspected "communist influences" in American society. Fueled by rumor and suspicion, the group "blacklisted" thousands of men and women in Hollywood, making it impossible for them to work. In response Hepburn defiantly issued a press statement attacking the committee, proclaiming that "the artist, since the beginning of time, has always expressed the aspirations and dreams of his people. Silence the artist and you have silenced the most articulate voice the people have."

When she was not endorsing a cause, however, Hepburn continued to avoid the press. She rarely gave interviews, and when she did, she often refused to answer most of the questions. Thus, along with her Oscars, she often won the less coveted Hollywood Women's Press Club Sour Apple award—for Most Uncooperative Actress of the Year.

But to Hepburn, it was the work, not the trappings of stardom, that mattered. Not that all her films were rewarding. After her tour of Australia, she costarred with comedian Bob Hope in an ill-fated farce, *The Iron Petticoat*, in 1956. A rehash of a famous 1939 Greta Garbo film, *Ninotchka*, it was the story of a pilot (Hepburn) who defects from Russia and eventually comes to love capitalism. Hope had his own writers doctor the script to beef up his role, at

Hepburn looks suitably severe in this still from The Iron Petticoat, *a mediocre film about a Soviet defector. Many of her scenes were cut to play up comedian Bob Hope's role.*

the expense of Hepburn's. After the movie flopped, its original screenwriter, Ben Hecht, not only publicly disclaimed it, but also apologized to Hepburn because her "magnificent comic performance has been blow-torched out of the film."

The late 1950s and early 1960s brought her more satisfying roles, beginning with *The Rainmaker* (1956). Hepburn played Lizzie Curry, an aging Kansas spinster who is wooed by a handsome con man (Burt Lancaster). The poignant drama earned Hepburn her seventh Academy Award nomination, as well as critical praise. *Time* magazine reported, "She holds the eye in scene after scene like a brilliant moth as she batters wildly about one or another light o' love."

Desk Set (1957), with Spencer Tracy was more lighthearted—a spoof on the computer age—and one more triumph. But Hepburn's stint with Shaw and Shakespeare had whetted her appetite for serious theater; and toward the close of the decade, she turned her attention to two of America's greatest playwrights, Tennessee Williams and Eugene O'Neill.

In 1959, she starred in a film version of one of Williams's short plays, *Suddenly Last Summer*, with Elizabeth Taylor and Montgomery Clift. The script was a shocking tale of incest and homosexuality, with Hepburn playing an evil character called Mrs. Venable.

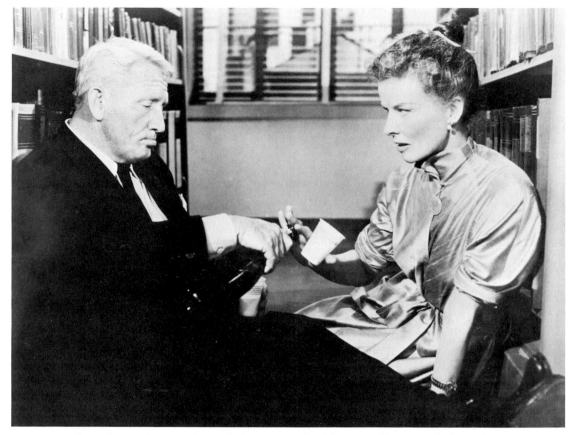

Tracy and Hepburn share a glass of champagne in this scene from Desk Set, *a breezy 1957 comedy about a woman whose job is threatened by a computer.*

During the shooting, tensions erupted on the set, prompting a display of Hepburn's famous high principles. Montgomery Clift was suffering from a variety of physical and psychological problems that were hampering his performance, and Hepburn thought director Joseph Mankiewicz was being needlessly brutal to him. Determined to see the project through, she kept quiet, but on the last day of filming she spat in Mankiewicz's face and refused to work with him ever again.

Despite the adverse working conditions, the film won Hepburn her eighth Oscar nomination and more rave reviews. Now a *Newsweek* critic wrote, "If she were any better, she'd be preposterous."

The Eugene O'Neill film was even more ambitious. The playwright was famous for his dark, psychological dramas, which had completely revolutionized American theater. *Long Day's*

Hepburn costarred with Elizabeth Taylor (right) in a film version of Tennessee Williams's play Suddenly Last Summer. *After seeing her performance, Williams praised Hepburn's "fineness of intelligence and sensibility."*

Journey into Night was one of O'Neill's lengthiest (four and a half hours long) and most difficult plays, with a controversial subject—drug addiction.

Hollywood set a higher premium on entertainment than art, so the movie had a very low budget. Its distinguished cast—Sir Ralph Richardson, Jason Robards, Jr., and Dean Stockwell—could be paid only tiny salaries. But as Hepburn later declared, "I've never been much interested in money

... I've gotten tremendous fees when the material was boring."

Her role as the morphine addict Mary Tyrone was extremely challenging. In one scene, she even had to roll around on the floor in a narcotic fog. But when she saw the final version, she called *Long Day's Journey into Night* "far damn well the best thing I've seen done"—and the critics agreed. It not only earned Hepburn her ninth Oscar nomination but *New Yorker* critic Pau-

Hepburn received her ninth Oscar nomination for her powerful portrayal of a morphine addict in the 1962 film version of Eugene O'Neill's play Long Day's Journey into Night.

line Kael said of her, "The most beautiful comedienne of the thirties and forties has become our greatest tragedienne."

Long Day's Journey into Night crowned a decade of magnificent achievements: four Academy Award nominations, several box office smashes, and celebrated interpretations of four of the greatest playwrights in the English language, Shaw, Shakespeare, Williams, and O'Neill. . . . Many actors would have been satisfied to have attained those heights in a lifetime, but Hepburn had done it in only 10 years. In a business that thrived on publicity, in which you were only as good as your last project, Hepburn's next move was a daring one: She dropped out of sight.

Concerned about Spencer Tracy's deteriorating health, Hepburn gave up her film and stage career for five years to serve as companion and nurse to the ailing actor.

SEVEN

On Her Own Again

Just after the completion of *Long Day's Journey into Night*, Katharine Hepburn's life was touched by tragedy. Her father, Thomas Hepburn, died late in 1962. In addition, Spencer Tracy's health, which had been damaged by a lifetime of heavy drinking, began to deteriorate rapidly.

Tracy had been hospitalized more than once, and in the summer of 1963, he was stricken with chest pains and shortness of breath as he and Hepburn were on their way to a Malibu, California, beach for a picnic. Hepburn immediately stopped the car to phone the fire department, who arrived with oxygen tanks. Her quick actions probably saved his life. With her characteristic sense of responsibility, Hepburn also called Tracy's estranged wife to tell her what had happened. As the two actors rode in the ambulance toward

the hospital, Tracy tried to reassure Hepburn with a show of humor. "Kate," he said, "isn't this a hell of a way to go to a picnic?"

It was after this frightening incident that Hepburn decided to retire from acting. She became Tracy's dedicated nurse, fussing over his diet and encouraging her reluctant patient to take the minimal exercise his doctor recommended. She sat up with him when he could not sleep and calmly administered oxygen when Tracy's failing heart required it.

Hepburn also tried to divert him from his troubles. She brought Tracy books to read and then engaged him in passionate, good-natured literary discussions. She arranged for friends to visit him. She borrowed new movies from the film studios for private screenings so that Tracy could keep up

Tracy and Hepburn go over their scripts on the set of Guess Who's Coming to Dinner?, *the controversial film that drew them out of retirement in 1967.*

with his colleagues' work. Somehow, she managed to do everything without ever making him feel like an invalid.

Tracy's ill health, and Hepburn's concern for him, kept both actors from working for several years (although Tracy did make a cameo appearance in 1963's *It's a Mad, Mad, Mad, Mad World*). Then, in late 1966, producer-director Stanley Kramer approached them with his idea for *Guess Who's*

Coming to Dinner? Tracy had worked with Kramer before, most notably in the acclaimed films *Inherit the Wind* and *Judgment at Nuremberg*. Tracy wanted to make at least one last film, especially one with a crew he respected and a theme he felt was important. One of his favorite sayings was comedian Joe E. Lewis's line, "You only live once—but if you work it right, once is *enough!*"

Tracy was scrupulously honest with Kramer in revealing his health problems, which might cause the movie to be left unfinished. But Kramer remained firm in his determination to work with Tracy. "The guy's got more moxie [courage] than any six I've ever known," Tracy told Garson Kanin. "I tell him my life expectancy is about seven and a half minutes, and he says, 'Action!' He's some kind of nut or saint. Or both."

As usual, *Guess Who's Coming to Dinner?* would be a Tracy-Hepburn movie—because, as usual, Tracy demanded top billing. Hepburn had never objected to taking a back seat to Tracy, believing he was the better actor and the bigger box office draw. In any case, Tracy was adamant about maintaining the star status he felt he had worked for and deserved. When his friend Garson Kanin suggested that, just once, he allow Hepburn to go first, Tracy replied, "This is a movie, chowderhead, not a lifeboat."

The billing order was one of the rules of their long, intimate partnership. During the filming, director Stanley Kramer had the chance to observe first-hand how that partnership worked. As he later recalled, Tracy would tell his beloved costar, "'Just do what the director guy tells you, will yah?' and she'd reply, humbly, 'All right.' She'd take anything from him. She'd take nothing from anybody else, from him everything."

Perhaps even more than in their previous eight movies together, in *Guess Who's Coming to Dinner?* Tracy and Hepburn were able to convey the intensity of their personal relationship on screen. One of the most poignant moments occurs near the end of the film, when Tracy delivers a speech informing the young couple that they would be lucky indeed if they had found a love as profound and lasting as the relationship he shares with Hepburn's character. At that instant, the movie make-believe drops away and the audience seems to be looking at Spencer Tracy in a very private moment, reflecting on his long love affair with his costar.

On June 10, 1967, two weeks after shooting was finished, Spencer Tracy died of heart failure. Toward the end, Hepburn had taken to sleeping in a small room near Tracy's so that she could hear him during the night. On the night he died, she heard him go into the kitchen. When she got up to check on him, she found him slumped at the kitchen table in front of a freshly poured glass of milk. As soon as she touched him, she knew he was gone.

Although she herself did not embrace any organized religion, Hepburn placed a Saint Christopher statue and Tracy's rosary beads in his coffin, out of respect for his strong Catholic faith. Then, consumed with grief, Hepburn went into seclusion. It was a devastating loss; as Garson Kanin reported, Hepburn would say of Tracy, "I'll miss him every day as long as I live." She told a journalist, "Any of the simple and pure things in life you can say about Spencer. He was like water, air, earth. He wasn't easily fooled—an unusual quality in the male. He was onto the human race—but with humor and understanding."

For months she remained withdrawn, but then in 1968, she plunged back into the work she had neglected during Tracy's long illness. That year she appeared as Eleanor of Aquitaine, the wife of Henry II of England (Peter O'Toole), in *The Lion in Winter*. Although she still mourned Tracy, her role as the medieval queen, reviewer Judith Crist wrote, "certainly crowns her career." Crist described Hepburn's Eleanor as "triumphant ... an aging beauty who can look her image in the eye, a sophisticate whose shrewdness is matched only by her humor." Hep-

burn was nominated for an Academy Award for Best Actress—her record-setting 11th—and won her third Oscar.

With her usual offhanded professionalism, Hepburn said of the honor, "It's one thing to win one of these things, it's another to deserve it. Sometimes the two happen at the same time. Then it's fine—I mean *fine*."

Hard work was proving to be a comfort and a tonic. Hepburn's next project was the film version of *The Madwoman of Chaillot*, a famous play by French writer Jean Giraudoux. Hepburn played the title role, an eccentric countess who is determined to save Paris from greed and corruption. When the producer unexpectedly replaced director John Huston with Bryan Forbes, the production suffered. One of Hepburn's costars, actor Paul Henreid, criticized Forbes's work, and later commented that, "As far as Kate was concerned, all he seemed to do was to make her smile and show her gums."

Although *The Madwoman of Chaillot* was not a critical success, Hepburn had enjoyed working on the unusual script. She looked for fresh challenges and soon received a very surprising of-

Hepburn joins in a cricket match on the set of The Lion in Winter. *The film's director, Anthony Harvey, said of Hepburn, "Working with her is like going to Paris at the age of 17 and finding everything is the way you thought it would be."*

Hepburn plays an eccentric idealist in a 1969 movie version of The Madwoman of Chaillot. *She had plunged back into work as a way to recover after Spencer Tracy's death.*

fer. Alan Jay Lerner, creator of the hit musical *My Fair Lady*, asked her to star in his newest play, a musical based on the life of Gabrielle "Coco" Chanel, the renowned French fashion designer. Hepburn was stunned by the prospect—for one thing, in all her years on stage, she had never even *seen* a Broadway musical. And being 60 years old, she exclaimed, "Good God! My feet. I couldn't do it. . . . Singing. Eight times a week. Probably dancing too. I'd go mad." After a pause, she concluded, "How fascinating!"

Chanel was the revolutionary designer who had first put stylish women in comfortable, practical clothes, rescuing them from the painful corsets and the tight skirts of the early 20th century. She was also a famous eccentric who, like Hepburn, loved men but shunned ˋconventional married life. Given the resemblance between the women, the role seemed tailor-made for Hepburn.

Even so, she was alarmed when Lerner suggested that she fly to Paris to meet Chanel, then in her eighties and still one of the most elegant women in the world. She told Lerner, "If I don't like her and I have to play her, it will be an agony." But she went; and after the meeting, Hepburn realized she'd left something behind in Chanel's apartment. She returned to find the *grande dame* of fashion "lying on the sofa, in her great big glasses and her big hat and her suit, very neat, having

Hepburn plays renowned fashion designer Coco Chanel in her only appearance in a Broadway musical. One critic said of her performance, "She does not submit to roles; she rules them."

a snooze! Now I *knew* I could play her. She was a human being!"

Hepburn finally did learn to sing (in a sort of distinguished croak) and to dance. What she lacked in technical skill she made up for in sheer nerve. Co-workers remember Hepburn scaling a six-foot backdrop in high heels to make an entrance on time after the revolving set failed to move. She played her role with gusto and, ultimately, managed to save what emerged as a mediocre production. Following a long standing ovation for the show's last night on Broadway on August 1, 1970,

Although she has won 4 Oscars and been nominated 11 times, Hepburn's only appearance at an Academy Awards ceremony came in 1974, when she presented her longtime friend, producer Lawrence Weingarten, with a special award.

Hepburn told the audience, "Well—I love you and you love me and that's that." Critics hailed her performance in *Coco*, and she was nominated for a Tony Award.

From Broadway, Hepburn took *Coco* on a national tour that began in her home town, Hartford, Connecticut. There, surprisingly, most of the critics lashed both the play and its star. One

night, when Hepburn returned to her family's home after a performance, her chauffeur, a woman who had apparently gone berserk, jumped out of a closet and attacked her with a hammer. Hepburn told a biographer, "We struggled, and went over and over, down the stairs. I never knew what her problem was." Hepburn's finger was badly injured in the battle. "Of course,

Wearing a hat from her Love Among the Ruins *costume, Hepburn hitches a ride from a classic Rolls Royce during a break in the filming of the 1975 television production.*

having a finger bitten off," Hepburn joked, was not as bad as "having my head bitten off by the home-town reviews!"

Her foray into musical theater had not dampened Hepburn's enduring love of great drama. In 1971 she appeared as Queen Hecuba in a film version of an ancient epic tragedy by Euripides, *The Trojan Women*. A movie version of *A Delicate Balance*, a drama by the maverick American playwright Edward Albee, followed in 1971; and in 1973, she made a television film of *The Glass Menagerie*, by her old friend Tennessee Williams. It was her first appearance in a production made for television, a medium she had always rejected. When asked why she decided to change her mind, she simply replied, "Curiosity killed the cat."

Other television programs followed. In 1975 she delivered an Emmy Award-winning performance in *Love Among the Ruins*, an impressive production directed by George Cukor and costarring Laurence Olivier. And in 1979, Hepburn collaborated for the last time with Cukor, the director who had launched her Hollywood career back in 1932, on a television production of Emlyn Williams's play *The Corn Is Green*.

And she continued to make films, in 1975 costarring with John Wayne in *Rooster Cogburn*. Although now past the age when most people retire, she was determined to do as much of her own stunt work as possible. She explained, "I haven't waited all these years to do a cowboy picture with John Wayne to give up a single minute of it now." She also loved the Oregon wilderness where the film was shot and spent her spare time running the rapids of the Rogue River in a small, inflatable boat—much to the horror of the company insuring the movie.

But for older actresses especially, good scripts were hard to find. As Hepburn approached her eighth decade, most of the parts she was offered were character roles—eccentric old ladies—rather than the starring roles an actress of Hepburn's stature would expect. In addition, although Hepburn was still slim, energetic, and beautiful, she was afflicted with a neurological disorder that made her hands and

head shake and her voice quaver like an old woman's. Hepburn was determined that her condition would not curtail her career, but it may indeed have cost her some roles.

So when Jane Fonda came to her in 1980 with the script for *On Golden Pond*, Hepburn was surprised and thrilled. *On Golden Pond* was the story of an elderly couple's attempt to enjoy a summer at a lake, despite family conflicts and the husband's illness. Fonda had purchased the movie rights to the play as a vehicle for herself and her father, whose off-screen lives mirrored the turbulent but ultimately loving relationship of the play's father and daughter.

Henry Fonda, himself in failing health, would portray the proud, ailing husband, and the strong-willed daughter would be played by Jane. Both Fondas agreed that Hepburn was the only choice for the feisty, resilient wife.

Hepburn and Henry Fonda had never met before, but they got on well together. "Working with Henry brings tears to my eyes," Hepburn told a reporter. "He is so sensitive, so giving as an actor. I've always admired him, of course, but working with him for the first time is a marvel." Fonda had compliments of his own for Hepburn.

The 66-year-old Hepburn insisted on doing her own stunt work when she costarred with John Wayne in a 1975 western called Rooster Cogburn.

Hepburn and actor Henry Fonda costarred in On Golden Pond, *shot in the New England countryside she had always loved.*

"What a joy it is acting with Katharine," he said. "She can play all the levels of a scene and always is able to add something so fresh with a slight gesture or look." Hepburn gave Fonda an old hat of Spencer Tracy's as a mark of her affection for him. Deeply touched, Fonda responded by painting a picture of the hat and giving it to Hepburn.

Together, Hepburn and Fonda created a deeply moving portrait of lovers touched by age. Audiences flocked to the theaters, and although some thought the film was overly sentimental, there was considerable praise for the two stars. *Time* magazine put Hep-burn and Fonda on the cover and proclaimed, "At last Kate and Hank!" Critic Richard Schickel said, "If people were allowed to vote on such matters, the pair would probably be grandparents to an entire nation." Although Academy Award nominations usually go to younger, more "romantic" stars, no one was surprised when both Henry Fonda and Katharine Hepburn were on the list of Oscar nominees.

But on Oscar night, March 19, 1982, Hepburn was thousands of miles away from Hollywood—in Washington, D.C., where she was starring in *West Side Waltz*, a comedy about the physical and psychological problems of aging, written for her by Ernest Thompson, the author of *On Golden Pond*. Not that Hepburn expected to win; she had already garnered an astonishing 11 nominations for Best Actress and had captured the award 3 times. But she had high hopes for Henry Fonda: Nominated many times in his distinguished professional life, he had never won an Oscar.

To Hepburn's delight, Henry Fonda was chosen Best Actor that night. Because his health had deteriorated dramatically in the past few months, Jane Fonda accepted the Academy Award for her father, who died later that year. But one of the biggest surprises of the evening came when it was announced that Hepburn had won an unprecedented fourth Academy Award. Hepburn modestly downplayed her achievement, telling journalists the next day, "These days you are so lucky if you get a good part." But as she had demonstrated time and time again, nearly every part was a good one—if Katharine Hepburn played the role.

Hepburn gets a kiss from singer Frank Sinatra during a 1986 tribute to Spencer Tracy, which marked the first time she spoke publicly about her romance with the late actor.

Hepburn had host Dick Cavett in stitches during a rare talk-show appearance in 1972. The audience was delighted by the opportunity to glimpse the private life of the celebrated actress.

An imposing Katharine Hepburn smolders by the fireplace in The Philadelphia Story.
Biographer Garson Kanin once said of her, "Katharine Hepburn is tall—not as tall as she thinks she is, but tall."

An American Legend

Certain images of Katharine Hepburn have become fixtures of 20th-century popular culture. Few movie fans will ever forget Hepburn as Tracy Lord in *The Philadelphia Story*, a formidable vision in tailored slacks and a severe black blouse, hands on hips, cheekbones jutting, a flinty look in her eye that convinces you she will take no prisoners. Hepburn was also memorable as Amanda Bonner in *Adam's Rib*, wearing a succession of severe yet stylish suits as she did battle in the courtroom, where she held the judge, the jury, and even her own husband in awe of her cutting competence and willingness to go to any extremes to win. Hepburn also made her mark as Rose Sayer, the stuffy missionary with an iron resolve who lets her hair down in *The African Queen*.

These images of Katharine Hepburn have both reflected and stimulated changes in the way we look at women today. From the time she first appeared on the screen in 1932, Hepburn has been spectacularly original. Unlike the coquettish sex symbols of the 1930s, she looked and behaved like a *real* American woman. In the 1950s, she resisted the prevailing stereotypes that other female stars portrayed—the helpless, sultry beauty or the wholesome suburban mother—to create heroines of real power. As she grew older she remained a public and critical success, well into her seventies, debunking the Hollywood dictum that a star had to be glamorous and young. As critic Pauline Kael has written, "At her best, her wit and nonconformity made ordinary heroines seem mushy, and her angular beauty made the round-faced ingenues look piggy and stupid.

Hepburn and actor Charles Boyer gaze longingly at one another in this love scene from Break of Hearts, *filmed in 1935.*

She was hard where they were soft—both in head and body."

This hardheadedness extended to her business dealings as well. While in her early twenties, she went to Hollywood on her own terms, dictating her own salary at a time when the "studio system" (the Hollywood machinery for manufacturing and manipulating "stars") was at its strongest. In the late 1930s she singlehandedly revived her flagging acting career by gambling on *The Philadelphia Story*—adding her own money to funds she had raised for the play—and by keeping hold of the film rights. Throughout her career, she rarely allowed a manager to make her decisions for her; and there have been innumerable stories about her ability to drive a hard bargain with studio executives.

Artistically, too, she did her best to call the shots, educating herself about every stage of film production. The directors she worked with often bridled at her insistence that scenes be done *her* way, but they ultimately came to respect her knowledge and her commitment to hard work. If she was a "difficult" perfectionist on the set, she was

Fusing intelligence, confidence, and beauty, Hepburn cut a striking figure as newspaper columnist Tess Harding in 1942's Woman of the Year.

no less hard on herself—always pushing to new heights of achievement, always the consummate professional.

She was no more compromising when it came to public relations. Rejecting conventional "star" glamour, she always dressed comfortably in her trademark slacks, topped by severely cut jackets and man-tailored coats. At a time when marriage and motherhood were judged the ultimate goals for women, she outspokenly maintained that neither was right for her. And in a Hollywood powered by gossip—often created by the studios to keep stars in the public eye—she fiercely defended her right to keep her personal life out of the headlines. In 1965, she even published an article, "The Right of Privacy: The Predicament of the Public Figure," in the *Virginia Law Review*. Using a punctuation style all her own, she wrote:

> In the beginning of my career—in 1932—I had a right to consider privacy my right—and so I fought for it—a wild and vigorous battle—I went to a great deal of trouble—I went way—way out of my way.... I used to go through the most elaborate schemes to avoid the press—I felt that nothing of my private life was any of their business—By the same token I did not feel that I could then appear in a public place.... These places were their territory—My territory was my own home—a friend's house—a private club—This is all very well—but then you have the public place on a private matter—the hospital—the church—the cemetery—where a public figure is forced by illness or death to use a public facility—It would seem that in such a case he or she should have the right to be protected from the peering eye of the outsider.

Part of her mania for privacy, certainly, was her desire to shield her married lover, Spencer Tracy, and his family from scandal. Despite the conservative spirit of her times, she maintained a personal and professional relationship with Tracy for 25 years. It was in her films with Tracy and, to some extent, in their offscreen personal life as well, that she approached most closely the traditional ideal of a submissive woman. She went on location with him, learned to fix rare steaks and strong coffee the way he liked them, and quit working at the peak of her career to care for him. In their films she always granted him higher billing than hers and always allowed his characters to win out in the end. But in those days, anything else would have been startling; in Hollywood, genuinely independent women (with a few notable exceptions, such as Mae West) were virtually unknown. Still, in many of her films, Hepburn managed to nudge audiences toward an acceptance of a new image of women as powerful individuals in their own right, entitled to the same respect as men.

For more than half a century, Hepburn has remained a fierce individualist, a symbol and an inspiration to many women and to an entire gener-

Despite her distinctive East Coast accent, Hepburn tackled Shakespeare's As You Like It.
Actress Tallulah Bankhead once commented, "Whenever I see Kate perform, at first I wonder
why she talks that way. And then when I come out of the theater, I wonder why everyone
doesn't talk like Kate."

With characteristic modesty, Katharine Hepburn once commented on her celebrity, "I'm a legend because I've survived over a long period of time. I'm revered rather like an old building."

Bryn Mawr president Mary Patterson McPherson welcomes Hepburn to the college's 1985 graduation ceremonies. Biographer Garson Kanin remarked, "As the years go by she does not lose her old admirers, she goes on gaining new ones."

ation of young actresses. Social activist and actress Jane Fonda has acknowledged her debt to Hepburn, expressing her awe at Hepburn's courageous independence. Borrowing the title of an upcoming film role, *McCall's* magazine named her its Woman of the Year in 1941: "We honor Katharine Hepburn as a woman, not actress, though surely she is much of both. Beauty, grace, talent, devotion—Miss Hepburn has the traditional feminine virtues in untraditional ways. She is a raving individual. We should have more like her."

The editors of *McCall's* were right: Out of all the characters she portrayed, Katharine Hepburn, the woman and the legend, is probably her greatest creation. Over the years, she adroitly overcame career setbacks, personal losses, and efforts to falsify her public image. She once said, "Two of an actress's greatest assets are love and pain. A great actress, even a good actress, must have plenty of both in her life." Hepburn has, but she has chosen to keep both to herself, using them only to enrich her art.

As Humphrey Bogart said of her after they worked together in Africa, "She fascinated me: *she kept to her course.* She was one of those curiously lucky aristocrats to whom life comes easily." Although Bogart's second statement is not accurate, it points to one of Hepburn's greatest attributes. Her legend arises not only from what she has accomplished, which is considerable, but also from her astonishing ability to make her achievements look easy.

KATHARINE HEPBURN'S SCREEN AND STAGE PERFORMANCES

FILMS

A Bill of Divorcement, 1932.
Christopher Strong, 1933.
Morning Glory, 1933.
Little Women, 1933.
Spitfire, 1934.
Break of Hearts, 1935.
The Little Minister, 1935.
Alice Adams, 1935.
Sylvia Scarlett, 1935.
Mary of Scotland, 1936.
A Woman Rebels, 1936.
Quality Street, 1937.
Stage Door, 1937.
Bringing Up Baby, 1938.
Holiday, 1938.
The Philadelphia Story, 1940.
Woman of the Year, 1942.
Keeper of the Flame, 1942.
Stage Door Canteen, 1943.
Dragon Seed, 1944.
Without Love, 1945.
Undercurrent, 1946.
Sea of Grass, 1947.
Song of Love, 1947.
State of the Union, 1948.
Adam's Rib, 1949.
The African Queen, 1951.
Pat and Mike, 1952.
Summertime, 1955.
The Iron Petticoat, 1956.
The Rainmaker, 1956.
Desk Set, 1957.
Suddenly Last Summer, 1959.
Long Day's Journey into Night, 1962.
Guess Who's Coming to Dinner?, 1967.
The Lion in Winter, 1968.
The Madwoman of Chaillot, 1969.
The Trojan Women, 1971.
A Delicate Balance, 1973.
Rooster Cogburn, 1975.
Olly Olly Oxen Free, 1978.

On Golden Pond, 1981.
The Ultimate Solution of Grace Quigley, 1984.
Love Affair, 1994.

TELEVISION MOVIES

The Glass Menagerie, 1973.
Love Among the Ruins, 1975.
The Corn Is Green, 1979.
Mrs. Delafield Wants to Marry, 1986.
The Man Upstairs, 1992.
This Can't Be Love, 1994.

PLAYS

The Czarina, 1928.
The Big Pond, 1928.
Death Takes a Holiday, 1928.
The Man Who Came Back, 1928.
A Month in the Country, 1929.
The Admirable Crichton, 1929.
Art and Mrs. Bottle, 1929.
A Romantic Young Lady, 1929.
The Animal Kingdom, 1931.
The Warrior's Husband, 1932.
The Lake, 1934.
Jane Eyre, 1937.
The Philadelphia Story, 1939.
Without Love, 1942.
As You Like It, 1951.
The Millionairess, 1952.
Measure for Measure, 1955.
The Taming of the Shrew, 1955.
The Merchant of Venice, 1955.
The Merchant of Venice, 1957.
Much Ado About Nothing, 1957.
Twelfth Night, 1960.
Antony and Cleopatra, 1960.
Coco, 1970.
A Matter of Gravity, 1976.
West Side Waltz, 1981.

FURTHER READING

Carey, Gary. *Katharine Hepburn.* New York: St. Martin's, 1983.

Dickens, Homer. *The Films of Katharine Hepburn.* New York: Citadel Press; 1973.

Edwards, Anne. *A Remarkable Woman.* New York: Random House, 1986.

Freedland, Michael. *Katharine Hepburn.* London: W. H. Allen, 1984.

Higham, Charles. *Kate: The Life of Katharine Hepburn.* New York: New American Library, 1981.

Kanin, Garson. *Tracy and Hepburn: An Intimate Memoir.* New York: Viking, 1971.

Latham, Caroline. *Katharine Hepburn: Her Films and Stage Career.* New York: Proteus Books, 1982.

Marill, Alvin H. *Katharine Hepburn.* New York: Pyramid Publications, 1973.

Shipman, Donald. *The Great Movie Stars: The Golden Years.* New York: Crown, 1970.

CHRONOLOGY

Nov. 8, 1909	Katharine Hepburn born in Hartford, Connecticut
1924–28	Attends Bryn Mawr College
1928	Is fired on opening night after landing her first role on Broadway in *The Big Pond*
Dec. 12, 1928	Marries Ludlow Ogden Smith; the couple separates after three weeks
1932	Stars in *The Warrior's Husband*, her first Broadway success; appears in her first film, *A Bill of Divorcement*
1933	Receives her first Academy Award for *Morning Glory*
1934	Divorces Ludlow Ogden Smith
1935	Stars in *Alice Adams*, which brings her a second Academy Award nomination
1938	Is branded "Box Office Poison" by the Independent Theater Owners of America
1939	Opens on Broadway in *The Philadelphia Story*
1940	Revives her movie career with the film version of *The Philadelphia Story*
1942	Begins relationship with Spencer Tracy during the filming of *Woman of the Year*
1949	Costars with Tracy in *Adam's Rib*
1951	Receives her fifth Academy Award nomination for *The African Queen*
1952	Appears in London and New York productions of *The Millionairess*
1955	Stars in *Summertime*; tours Australia performing in three Shakespeare plays
1957	Costars with Tracy in *Desk Set*
1959	Stars in *Suddenly Last Summer*, a film based on a Tennessee Williams play
1962	Appears in *Long Day's Journey into Night*, for which she receives her ninth Academy Award nomination
1967	Returns to screen after a five-year absence to deliver an Academy Award–winning performance in *Guess Who's Coming to Dinner?*
June 10, 1967	Spencer Tracy dies
1968	Hepburn receives her third Academy Award for *The Lion in Winter*
1970	Makes her Broadway musical debut in *Coco*
1981	Receives her fourth Academy Award for *On Golden Pond*
1994	Returns to the big screen after a 10–year absence in *Love Affair*, with Warren Beatty and Annette Bening
1995	Publishes autobiography *Me: Stories of My Life*

INDEX

PICTURE CREDITS

The Bettmann Archive: pp. 12, 15, 16, 18, 29, 32, 34, 37, 42, 43, 45, 46, 48, 52, 53, 55, 56, 58, 62, 65 (top), 65 (bottom), 73, 86, 90, 91, 95, 96, 98, 100, 101; Bryn Mawr College: pp. 24, 104; Museum of Modern Art/Film Stills Archive: pp. 39, 50, 57, 75, 80, 92, 97; New York Public Library: (Frontispiece), pp. 49, 105; Springer/Bettmann Film Archive: pp. 25, 26, 54 (top), 54 (bottom), 61, 63, 70–71, 78, 79, 81, 82, 104; UPI/Bettmann Newsphotos: pp. 14, 20, 22, 28, 31, 36, 40, 44, 66, 69, 74, 76, 83, 88–89, 93, 97.

Caroline Latham's books include *Katharine Hepburn: Her Film and Stage Career, The David Letterman Story, Carol Burnett: Funny Is Beautiful,* and *How to Live With a Man.* She has also written biographies of Michael Jackson, Bill Cosby, and Priscilla Presley, and is co-author of *Life with Rose Kennedy.* Latham resides in Hudson, New York.

❖   ❖   ❖

Matina S. Horner is president of Radcliffe College and associate professor of psychology and social relations at Harvard University. She is best known for her studies of women's motivation, achievement, and personality development. Dr. Horner serves on several national boards and advisory councils, including those of the National Science Foundation, Time Inc., and the Women's Research and Education Institute. She earned her B. A. from Bryn Mawr College and Ph.D. from the University of Michigan, and holds honorary degrees from many colleges and universities, including Mount Holyoke, Smith, Tufts, and the University of Pennsylvania.